STORIES
by WILLIMON

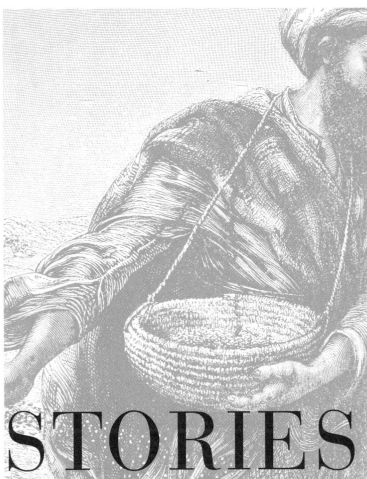

STORIES

by WILLIMON

Abingdon Press
Nashville

The Sower

[Jesus] said many things to [the crowds] in parables:

"A farmer went out to scatter seed. As he was scattering seed, some fell on the path, and birds came and ate it. Other seed fell on rocky ground where the soil was shallow. They sprouted immediately because the soil wasn't deep. But when the sun came up, it scorched the plants, and they dried up because they had no roots. Other seed fell among thorny plants. The thorny plants grew and choked them. Other seed fell on good soil and bore fruit, in one case a yield of one hundred to one, in another case a yield of sixty to one, and in another case a yield of thirty to one. Everyone who has ears should pay attention."

Jesus's disciples came and said to him, "Why do you use parables when you speak to the crowds?"

Jesus replied, "Because they haven't received the secrets of the kingdom of heaven, but you have. For those who have will receive more and they will have more than enough. But as for those who don't have, even the little they have will be taken away from them. This is why I speak to the crowds in parables: although they see, they don't really see; and although they hear, they don't really hear or understand. What Isaiah prophesied has become completely true for them:

> You will hear, to be sure, but never understand;
>
> and you will certainly see but never recognize what you are seeing.
>
> For this people's senses have become calloused,

and they've become hard of hearing,

and they've shut their eyes

so that they won't see with their eyes

or hear with their ears

or understand with their minds,

and change their hearts and lives that I may heal them.

"Happy are your eyes because they see. Happy are your ears because they hear. I assure you that many prophets and righteous people wanted to see what you see and hear what you hear, but they didn't."

Matthew 13:3-17

Contents

Foreword

One of the best things about working for Jesus is his stories. If you like your gods theoretical or immediately practical, apophatic and aloof, obvious and orderly, direct and straightforward, then go worship obviousness and practicality rather than Jesus. On the other hand, if you delight in being teased, cajoled, surprised, jolted, and tossed about, there's nobody better than Jesus when he's on a roll with his stories.

"Tell us who God really is," we asked. "You're not the god we craved or expected."

And Jesus replied (as is so typical) not with a lecture or an enunciation of biblical principles but with a story: "A farmer went out to scatter seed..."

Both Mark and Matthew say that Jesus said nothing except in parables (Mark 4:34; Matt 13:34). In word and deed, he was a parable: the storyteller become the story. Just as preachers quickly learn there's no better way to bore into the brains of our congregations than narrative, our Creator knew that the best way to get to creatures is through stories.

Everything starts with a story: "When God began to create the heavens and the earth—the earth was without shape or form, it was dark over the deep sea,...God said, 'Let there be light'" (Gen 1:1-3).

Sowers

Sowers are people of great faith. To dare to plant a seed is to put oneself at the mercy of the future, to risk farming failure, to hazard your work to factors beyond your control. Harvest is hoped for, never guaranteed.

Still, storytellers keep talking, keep sowing, persist in making something out of nothing but words, all in the faith that someone will listen, that somebody out there is dying to hear your story and make it their own. All the narrator can do is tell the story, sling the seed, and then wait to be surprised by the soul in which it takes root.

Storytelling in Jesus's name is done in faith that God is determined to have the last word, in hope that nothing—our indifference, sin, or idolatry—shall defeat God's determination to get through to us. Every preacher clings to the hope that the prophet's words are true: "My word...does not return to me empty" (Isa 55:11).

My preaching life has been an illustration of Paul's truth: *one sows and another harvests*. It's rather remarkable that stories Jesus told so long ago, to people so unlike us, amid a culture so different from ours, should have resonance today. Though I've made a fairly good living retelling Jesus's tales, Jesus was crucified, in great part, because people didn't like the stories he told. I'm a bit ashamed that my retelling of Jesus's provocative stories has cost me so little. Still, while I've got breath, I will testify that preaching is a great way to go, experiencing (not as often as I'd like but often enough to keep me at it) Jesus speaking through me so that he might have his say among his gathered people.

Because the gospel is news that you cannot tell yourself, God appoints sowers, people who are willing to risk telling others the gospel truth that was told to them. How will they hear without a preacher (Rom 10:14)—somebody with the guts to tell us a story on Sunday about something we've spent all week avoiding? To be Christian is to realize that you are the empty-handed recipient of this faith; we have nothing that we have not received, all of us utterly dependent upon another to tell us a true story about God.

Thus, Jesus not only told stories but called and commissioned others to tell his stories that we can't make up for ourselves. Down through the ages, the Sower has produced a great company of sowers, urging his disciples to pray "the Lord of the harvest to send out laborers into his harvest," lamenting that "the harvest is plentiful, but the laborers are few" (Luke 10:2 NRSV).

Though few, there have been enough tellers of Jesus's tales to get the job done. *Seminary* literally means "seedbed," where novices learn to tell the old, old story in such a way that, by the grace of God, it becomes somebody's news. No corner of creation has been immune from the words of someone summoned to say, "And God said..."

I've watched a pastor stand before a small, rural church and tell people truth they didn't want to hear, a story that implies that Jesus Christ is Lord (therefore The Donald is not), attempting to weave their narcissistic, deceitful little lives into a grand narrative of God's redemption. I'm in awe of her obedience to the prophetic command to *sow the seeds of justice*.

Seeds

Jesus's seminal stories are not the main thing; they are the way toward the main thing. We don't worship his tales; we worship the Teller of the tales. Jesus's words are seeds awaiting germination, taking time to take root (John 12:24). Patience is required.

As in his story of the sower and the seed, most of what Jesus says is wasted. The majority of the seed falls upon barren ground, is consumed by birds, or worldly concerns, squandered, choked by weeds. Hearing, we don't hear, seeing, we don't see. The Sower is recklessly willing to imperil good seed in the confidence that though much is wasted on the likes of us, those few kernels that bear fruit make the risks and losses of sowing worthwhile.

When you listen to one of his stories and reply, "Sorry. I just don't get it," Jesus's typical response is, "Try this: There was a woman who hid a little yeast in a huge lump of dough... Not helpful? Here's another: There was a father who had two sons..."

Why are so many of my stories humorous? Blame it on Jesus. I don't get how some can listen to Jesus and not hear his humor. Rather than judge us as we deserve, how gracious of God to enjoy having a laugh at our expense. Sensing the gap between God and us servants of God, we can either laugh or cry. Jesus, it appears from his stories, votes for laughter.

What can you say about a God who, in response to our stuffed-shirt self-righteousness, told another joke about people who think they are righteous and look down on everybody else (Luke 19:9)? You can say God was in Christ, blissfully reconciling us laughable, silly, so silly sinners to himself (2 Cor 5:19).

Senses

As a preacher, I marvel that Jesus doesn't mind wasting his best stories on us. I like my sermons to be effective, pray for my listeners to mutter, "Never have I had God rendered so clearly and memorably as in your sermon."

Jesus is astoundingly free of the compulsion to put his truth on the bottom shelf, to beat you over the head with obvious meaning. He never asks us to write anything down. Rarely explains or ties up his stories with a bow whereby you can say triumphantly, "I got it!"

More typically, his parables lead us to mutter, "It got me."

Jesus risks misunderstanding, as if getting the point, figuring him out, fully grasping the intent of his telling is not the point. Many's the time I've retold one of Jesus's more outrageous parables (and there are many), and have been forced to rhetorically ask the congregation, "Are you sure you want to follow a Savior who dares tell stories like this to people like us?"

In twenty years as preacher at Duke, when some student emerged from the chapel scratching his head and complaining, "I just didn't get the point," I've responded, "How high did you score on the SAT?...1350? Well, that's just average around here. I'll tell Jesus that his story succeeded in befuddling and stupefying an oh-so-smart Duke sophomore. He'll be thrilled!"

Most of those who first heard Jesus's parables were confused by them. So are we. His exasperated first disciples complained, "Why must you speak in these riddles?" (Matt 13:10, paraphrased).

Jesus replied by quoting Isaiah: people have shut their eyes and closed their ears; looking they don't see; listening they don't hear. Our intellectual defenses against God are well-developed. Fortunately for us, Jesus liked nothing better than healing the blind or opening the ears of the deaf. No better way to do that than through a story that begins, "God's realm is like..."

Parables conceal and reveal. In Matthew, Jesus says that he tells parables so people can better understand the realm of God. Stories open our eyes, unstop our ears.

In Mark 4:12, Jesus says just the opposite: the purpose of parables is "so that they can look and see but have no insight, and they can hear but not understand. Otherwise, they might turn their lives around and be forgiven." They thought they were spiritually perceptive until I smack 'em with my stories. My parables strike them deaf and blind and rob them of their damnable certitude.

Again, sorry if you must have your Saviors obvious. Don't ask Jesus not to be sly or obtuse.

A good parable's ambiguity and thickness begs interpretation. Few can sit by passively when Jesus aims a parable our way. Our interpretive devices immediately go into action. We try to find the hero of the story, hoping that hero will look like us. We attempt a sorting of the good from the bad—a notoriously difficult task when it comes to Jesus's stories. He loves antiheroes, which is maybe one reason why we, the unheroic, so often exclaim, "Hey, you're talking about me!"

Parables must be unpacked, pondered, argued, chewed, and interpreted. In telling his truth parabolically, Jesus requires us to accept some of the responsibility for the making of meaning.

Figuring out a story of Jesus fosters humility, forcing us to go hat in hand to the Holy Spirit, pleading, "Sorry, I just don't get it. Mind helping me with some of the hermeneutical lifting?"

I've been preaching for nearly fifty years; Jesus still manages to shock me with a text. Sharing my surprise with a congregation can make for an interesting sermon. It also means that I've got to toss out the last two sermons I earlier preached on that story—my beloved previous interpretation trashed by Jesus.

I've had the embarrassing experience of preaching at least five sermons on the Dishonest Steward (my label; Jesus doesn't entitle his stories), Luke 16:1-15, and have ended by confessing, "I can read this in the original Greek, I've got at least twenty books on my shelf that purport to explain this parable, and God help me, I still am unsure why Jesus told it."

After battering them all day with a barrage of parables, Jesus asked his disciples, "Have you understood all these things?" (Matt 13:51).

They gleefully responded, "Sure! We get it."

They lied.

Secrets

Still, the meaning of *metaphor* is to shine light on something, to promote understanding. I can't believe Jesus's purpose in telling stories was to make us look stupid; we don't need his stories for that. Mark's favorite designation for Jesus was "Rabbi," teacher. Jesus really wants to share the mysteries of the kingdom (Mark 4:11). Trouble is, the subject matter Jesus taught required a willingness to endure pedagogical failure. His stories are no more obscure and difficult than they need to be, considering Jesus's peculiar way, truth, and life.

Jesus responds to his disciples' plea, "How come you tell so many stories?" not only by reminding them that Isaiah warned that most hearers would be clueless but also by charitably congratulating them for having received "the secrets of the kingdom."

Refusing to waste time speculating on why many did not understand his parabolic teaching (everybody knows that human stupidity is ubiquitous), Jesus congratulates his gaggle of followers by saying, "Happy are your eyes because they see. Happy are your ears because they hear. I assure you that many prophets and righteous people wanted to see what you see and hear what you hear, but they didn't" (Matt 13:16-17).

We disciples of Jesus may not be the brightest candles in the box, but at least we happy few know a true story when we hear one. It's humbling to know that Jesus entrusts us with divine mysteries that are unknown to nine out of ten average Americans.

While I don't believe that Jesus was parabolic in order to dumb down for the agrarian rubes of Galilee—if that was his intention, the vast misunderstanding and outright hostility that he received for his storytelling prove it didn't work—I do believe that his parables offer unique access to the mysteries of God.

When questioned about his relentless storytelling, Jesus said that he told stories for the same reason as Isaiah, "*I'll declare what has been hidden since the beginning of the world.*" The primary purpose of Jesus's stories is not to make us feel fatuous but to reveal to us the truth about God. In Jesus and his stories, God loves us enough to go public with God's secrets. Refusing to go coy or ethereal, a hazy blur or vague feeling, God in Christ lets us in on the public secret of who God is and what God is up to, alluring us, turning narration into vocation: Now that I've let you in on who God really is, don't you want to hitch onto God's vast retake of what belongs to God? Follow me!

Somebody named Mark, sometime during the first century, somewhere in the Levant, had to invent a literary form previously unknown in order to tell the whole truth about Jesus. Biography, sort of; travel saga, in a way, Mark's Gospel is an extended story, a distinctively narrative way of presenting the meaning of a unique sort of Messiah. Something about Jesus—who he was and what he was up to—just couldn't be conveyed any other way than through this rambling travelogue replete with excursions such as, "He told a parable to those who trusted in their own righteousness and despised everybody else..." or, "Once there was a rich man who..."

In my ministry, God moved me from first-rate frat party fabulist, to Southern storyteller, to seminarian raconteur, to pulpit wit. Not all have approved of God's gift of narrative to me. "You told one story too many today," groused a grande dame post-sermon. "I need your advice, but I don't have time for all the damn stories," said an anxious undergraduate at the beginning of our pastoral counseling session. Some random student dismissed my class at Duke Divinity as no more than "story time with Will." Ungrateful wretches.

My late friend Stuart Henry said of my work, "Give Will a wilted daisy, a faded larkspur, and when he is done with his story, it's 'a riot of delphinium.'"

Some of my tendency to tell stories is due to my having been raised by a storytelling people who managed poverty, misfortune, and mortality by telling tales. Even the worst luck could be improved with a good story. Nothing is lost among a tribe of narrators. Good times were made better if there was someone to tell a story that, in the telling, transformed drab, prosaic Southern reality into fantastic fairy tale and fable.

It's high time for me at last to get to my point:

I tell so many stories because of Jesus.

Will Willimon

Part One

Sowers

Just as the rain and the snow come down from the sky and don't return there without watering the earth, making it conceive and yield plants and providing seed to the sower and food to the eater, so is my word that comes from my mouth; it does not return to me empty. Instead, it does what I want, and accomplishes what I intend.

Isaiah 55:10-11

This is a true saying, that one sows and another harvests.

John 4:37

Those who make peace sow the seeds of justice by their peaceful acts.

James 3:18

1

Good Sowers

On Sunday morning, after I'm done preaching at Duke Chapel and have retired to my appointed perch—the seat behind the second sopranos, where I blend into the woodwork—I often look up at the stained-glass window high above and across from me that depicts Moses. Only the second sopranos and I can see it. The window shows scenes from Moses's life: the child raised by royalty, the angry defender of the oppressed, the liberator, the lawgiver, the leader of Israel to the promised land.

But often—at about 11:45 a.m.—the sun highlights one scene more than the rest. It's the last event in Moses's ministry, when God prevents him from entering Canaan. Yahweh lets Moses get to the door but does not allow him to cross the threshold with Israel. Whether the artist who created these windows intended to force the preacher to ponder that scene week in, week out, I do not know. But I have memorized it in detail. As I look at the end of Moses's ministry, I am reminded of my own ministry.

A lot goes unfinished. Much of pastoral life is spent on the verge, at the door. Preaching takes the congregation to the threshold, but what lasting good does it do?

As I recently worked on a book on ministerial burnout, on why pastors call it quits, I was impressed that preaching, a central pastoral activity, is a major source of pastoral disillusionment. It's such a fragile art. Much of the time it takes to prepare a sermon is invisible—and so are the results. No one can demonstrate empirically verified outcomes of "good" preaching. And that's a problem in a world that worships results.

For me and for the sopranos, we must, like Moses, be content with planting while leaving the harvest for others. They sing, I preach, and

God only knows where it all leads, what land of promise will be opened through our ministry.

A man I know who works with teachers says the ones who are best able to keep at it over the years are those "who are good sowers rather than good reapers." Teachers and preachers must find meaning enough in the act of planting the seed and not have need to be there for the harvest.

If we preachers or choir members or Sunday school teachers are going to persevere at Christian ministry, we will do so only by having confidence that God really does convey treasure through us earthen vessels. God puts us to good purposes. Even though we may not understand God's plans, even though we may not enter the promised land of concrete results and visible fulfillment, we can boldly announce the message of the ultimate triumph of God's good purposes to those in exodus, going from here to there.

The Christian Ministry,
March–April 1989

2
Which One of You?

A farmer goes forth to sow, carefully, meticulously preparing the ground, removing rocks and weeds, sowing one seed six inches from another...

No! This farmer goes out and begins slinging seed.

A dragnet full of sea creatures is hauled into the boat. Sort the catch, separating the good from the bad? No. The Master is more impressed by the size of the haul than by the quality of the catch. One day, not today, it shall be sorted.

A field is planted with good seed. But when the seed germinates, the field is full of weeds growing alongside the wheat.

"An enemy has done this!" cries the farmer. Enemy, my foot. You get an agricultural mess when your idea of sowing is to so carelessly sling seed.

Should we cull the wheat from the weeds? "No, good plants or bad, I just love to see things grow," says the casual farmer.

Someday the Master will judge good from bad, weeds from wheat, sort out the righteous from the unrighteous, but not today.

So, here's a farmer and a fisherman who are more into heedless sowing, miraculous growing, and reckless harvesting than in taxonomy of the good and the bad, the worthwhile from the worthless, the saved from the damned.

Which one of you, having lost one sheep will not abandon the ninety-nine sheep (who lack the creativity to roam), leaving them to fend for themselves in the wilderness, and beat the bushes until you find the one lost sheep? Which one of you will not put that sheep on your shoulders like a child and say to your friends, "Come party with me. I found my sheep!"?

To which your friends would say, "Congratulations. You just lost most of your flock who wandered away while you were fixated on finding the one who wandered."

Which one of you would not do that?

Which of you women, if you lose a quarter, will not rip up the carpet and strip the house bare of heavy appliances, and when you have found your lost coin, run into the street and call to your neighbors, "Come party with me. I found my quarter!"?

Which one of you would not do that?

And which of you fathers, having two sons, the younger of whom leaves home, blows all your hard earned money on booze and bad women, then comes dragging back home in rags, will not throw the biggest bash this town has ever seen, shouting, "This son of mine was dead but is now alive!"?

Which one of you dads would not do that?

And which of you, journeying down the Jericho Road, upon seeing a perfect stranger lying in the ditch half dead, bleeding, would not risk your life, put the injured man on the leather seats of your Jaguar, take him to the hospital, max out your credit cards paying for his recovery, and more?

Which of you travelers would not do that?

None of us would behave so unseemly, recklessly, and extravagantly. These are not stories about us. *They are stories about God.*

Who Will Be Saved?,
Abingdon Press, 2008

3
Don't Take It Back

He owned a hardware store, and he was a member of my church. Someone had warned me about him when I moved there. "He's usually quiet," they said, "but be careful." People still recalled the Sunday in 1970 when, in the middle of the sermon (the previous preacher's weekly diatribe against Nixon and the Vietnam War), he had stood up from where he was sitting, shook his head, and walked right out. So, I always preached with one eye on my notes and the other on him. He hadn't walked out on a sermon in more than ten years. Still, a preacher can never be too safe.

You can imagine my fear when one Sunday, having waited until everyone had shaken my hand and left the narthex, he approached me, gritting his teeth and muttering, "I just don't see things your way, preacher."

I moved into my best mode of non-defensive defensiveness, assuring him that my sermon was just one way of looking at things, and that perhaps he had misinterpreted what I said, and even if he had not, I could very well be wrong and er, uh…

"Don't you back off with me," he snapped. "I just said that your sermon shook me up. I didn't ask you to take it back. Stick by your guns—if you're a real preacher."

Then he said to me, with an almost desperate tone, "Preacher, I run a hardware store. Since you've never had a real job, let me explain it to you. Now, you can learn to run a hardware store in about six months. I've been there *fifteen years*. That means that all week, nobody talks to me like I know anything. I'm not like you, don't get to sit around and read books and talk about important things. It's just me and that hardware store. Sunday morning and your sermons are all I've got. Please, don't you dare take it back."

"The Unfettered Word," sermon, Duke
University Chapel, October 15, 1989

4

Told You Sow

We had predicted it. At age fourteen she was on the rear end of a Honda, screaming up and down the street as if it were Daytona. "She will end up bad," we said. At fifteen I could tell, by the empty beer cans in my front yard the next day, what kind of weekend she had wasted. "They're just going to have to take her in hand," I said. "She's headed for trouble."

More than once, on those Saturday nights, her car radio electrified my sleep, sending me hurtling through space at 3 a.m. "People like that are a menace to society," we declared. Then at sixteen, there was a story in the papers, the trial, and she was sent away for a year at the Youth Correctional Institution. "We told you so," we said. "Only a matter of time," we agreed. While there, she gave birth to the child she was carrying.

The day of reckoning came. I was cutting my hedge at the time. I could see them, though. Cars began gathering about ten or eleven that morning. Loud music coming from the house. People came and went, bringing baskets of food, dishes, stacks of plates. Chairs were put out on the lawn. The music grew louder. Finally, a car pulled up. People came pouring out of the house and huddled around the car. Everybody oohing and aahing. I was hacking at the hedge, cutting it down to the roots by this time. Some kind of little basket, decorated with pink ribbons, was unloaded. Everyone paraded behind it into the house. I watched them from my now-sparse hedge. Before going in, my neighbor had the nerve to stand on the porch and yell, "Hey, she's home, and the baby too. Come on over and join us. We're having a party!"

Who? Me? Humph! I'm a Christian!

"Are you resentful because I'm generous?" (Matt 20:15)

"Graciousness and Grumbling,"
sermon, Northside United Methodist Church,
September 20, 1981

The Limits of Care: A Fable

"You are such a loving, caring pastor," he said.

"Thank you," she said.

"Sad to say, not all of the pastors we've had in the past were like you," he said.

"Thanks, but why did you want me to meet you here?" she asked. "It's a beautiful spot but a bit unusual location for a conversation."

"Why Summit Park? Well, it's because this place, this cliff overlooking town, the view from up here, has become an obsession for me. I just can't get it out of my head. Thought that maybe you could help."

"Help? An 'obsession'?" she asked. "In what way?"

"It's kinda hard to talk about. But you are always so affirming and are such a good, open listener. For the longest time I've had this urge to come up here and jump off this cliff. Just to see what happens," he said.

"What? 'See what happens'? Are you serious?" she exclaimed.

"I've got to say that I didn't expect you'd react in that way," he said.

"You could die! At the least you'd be severely injured. How on earth did you get the idea to throw yourself off this cliff?" she asked, looking around to see if anyone was nearby.

"I don't see it as 'throwing myself' over this cliff. Just sort of walk to the edge and see what's next. As you know, I've always been a lucky guy," he chatted, matter-of-factly. "I'm a real risk-taker. Hang gliding. Surfing when I was younger. Lately, my life has been getting a little stale. I thought the experience would be a real rush."

"No! Why would you want to injure yourself in this horrible way?"

"Pastor, far be it from me to remind you of scripture, but didn't Jesus say somewhere, 'God will give his angels care over you'?"

"No! Satan said that, not Jesus, when Satan was attempting to get Jesus to do just what you're talking about. And Jesus refused."

"I dunno. Maybe Satan is behind my wanting to do this. Maybe not. Who are you to judge? You know what they say, 'No pain, no gain.' I've got a real sense of adventure in me, love to live on the edge, as they say, so..."

"You're talking crazy!" she said. "Scary."

"I gotta say that I'm kinda hurt that you are not showing me much empathy," he said as he rose and moved toward the guardrail.

"Wait!" she shouted while looking around for help. "Don't do this to yourself."

They were the only two people in the park at that time of day.

"I'm disappointed that you haven't come up with a really convincing reason for why I shouldn't do what I'm feeling led to do. To soar, to experience bliss, to feel the joy of finally cutting loose and..."

"No!" was all that she could muster. She reached for his arm to restrain him, but he easily pulled away.

"I came here seeking your help. If you can't talk me out of this, whatever happens to me will always be on your conscience," he said as he stepped up and balanced himself precariously on the rail. "If you were really sincere about trying to help people, then I wouldn't be in this fix."

"You don't have to do this. Let's keep talking," she pled.

"Why? What good would that do? I've listened; you've talked. You haven't helped," he said as he looked out over the expanse of the valley far below.

"If you jump, it's your decision, not mine," she said. "Please don't do this to yourself."

"Why not? You are the most caring person I know. It's your job. Yet you haven't helped. It's your decision to have me on your conscience," were his last words as he leapt over the rail and instantly passed from view.

Shaken, she went back to her car to phone the authorities. Before she said to herself, *I decide to be their pastor, not their savior.*

With gratitude to Rabbi Edwin H. Friedman

6

Kleptomania Homiletica

Jesus said it; I believe it; that settles it. "Give to those who ask, and don't refuse those who wish to borrow from you" (Matt 5:42). Preachers get by only with a little help from generous friends.

A few years ago, I got a call from a reporter in the Northeast. "What is your position on preachers plagiarizing the work of other preachers?" she asked.

"Oh, I guess Craig Barnes has been whining about my lifting some of his material," I said, with contempt. "His vast web footprint begs for borrowing."

"No. This week a prominent pastor in the city will be removed from his pulpit because he's been caught downloading some of your sermons from Duke Chapel. Re-preaching. Word for word. The laity discovered it. In fact, a layperson has been secretly handing out copies of your sermons to other laity on the last two Sundays. They sit there in the service and follow along. Caught him red-handed. Don't you think the preacher should have at least changed the titles?" she asked.

Sometimes I despise laity.

Stephen Colbert employs something like twenty writers to help him come up with a nightly ten-minute monologue on Trump. It's nuts to think that I, much less any preacher who went to a seminary not as good as mine, can come up with a weekly sermon on Jesus, solo. An accountant can be solitary, keeping her eyes on her own work, refusing to ask for help, and do double entry bookkeeping just fine. But no preacher can afford to work alone.

If you are going to define and then condemn sermonic plagiarism, then you must come up with a definition of stealing that's so broad and charitable as to be meaningless. Source critics tell us that Luke and

Matthew routinely ripped off Mark. The Bible is better for it. What if Matthew had not said to Mark, "Let me see your Gospel. I think I can work this up into something mighty fine," or Mark had refused Matthew with, "Hey, it's my intellectual property"?

I define "heresy" as the arrogant attempt to be theologically original, breaking free of the resources of the *communio sanctorum*, refusing dependency on the "great company of preachers" (Ps 68:11), going rogue.

"Loved your sermon!" a woman gushed as she emerged from Duke Chapel after service one Sunday. "Loved it when Tom Long preached that sermon here in April, 1991. Shouldn't you at least have transposed some of the details?"

Laity!

For years I've written for *Pulpit Resource*, filling it with material to help pastors get going on next Sunday's sermon.

"Aren't you worried that some unscrupulous pastors may simply preach your sermons verbatim from *Pulpit Resource*?" critics ask.

I wish. As long as they do it with a Southern accent. Better my sermons than Adam Hamilton's, I say.

Jean Valjean stole bread only to feed his starving children. Me too. Kleptomania, the inability to refrain from stealing, is usually done for reasons other than personal use or financial gain, says the *DSM*. Stealing isn't really stealing if it's done unselfishly for the good of my neighbor. I've never taken anything from any preacher that was not done in service to my listeners. My sermonic borrowing is an indication of how much I love my people.

Sure, Ephesians says, "Let the thief no longer steal, but rather let him labor, doing honest work with his own hands." Cite that passage to rebuke me and I'll insist that you quote the rest of the verse: "So that they will have something to share with whoever is in need" (Eph 4:28, paraphrased). I took Tom Long's story of a group of men standing under an oak tree at his home church in Georgia, moved all of them to a larger church and a dogwood in South Carolina, and nobody was the worse for it. I doubt Tom preached that story to more than a couple of hundred; I've shared it with two thousand Baptists in Canada and they ate it up. I'm sure Tom would be flattered that his work did good all the way up in Canada. It's not stealing if you can improve on what you took.

As I've always said, "Don't just borrow sermon material; steal it." Picky you responds, "Hey, Picasso said that, not you. To quote more accurately, the great artist actually said this to his fellow artists, 'Good artists copy; great artists steal.'" Well, it turns out that Picasso likely never said that at all, but if he did, he likely stole it from T. S. Eliot who said, "Immature poets imitate; mature poets steal; bad poets deface what they take, and good poets make it into something better." Take that, all you fastidious OCDs who are always demanding attribution.

You say, "Hey, isn't that a story from David Buttrick?" I'll say, "I have no idea how that got in my bag."

Stanley Hauerwas said, "If you think you've had an original thought, it means that you forgot where you read it." Or maybe Oscar Wilde said that. Benjamin Franklin? Who cares? Hey, how do you know that *I* didn't say it?

Walt Brueggemann had a great story about a woman in a wheelchair and his meaningful conversation with her. All I did was take Walt's seat in that hospital room, have her retell the story to me, repackage her touching vignette, retell it with a Southern accent, connect it with a text from Genesis rather than the Psalms, and work it up into a more moving illustration than Walt's. And who was the worse for it? I can't help it if Walt, being from the Midwest, is not as good at storytelling as I. Just trying to help Walt obey Matthew 5:42.

When possible, if you are going to snatch something from a fellow preacher, it's usually good to ask in advance, but not always. I apologized for preaching an illustration of Jana Childers's, and she generously said,

"I don't care. I don't need it anymore." Then Jana spoiled it by saying, "I don't even believe that anymore. It's a sappy story anyway. Take it; it's yours."

"Do you mind if I borrow that little thing about the addict and the priest for my sermon on Good Friday?" I asked Nadia Bolz-Weber, "At my age I'm having increased difficulty kicking butt in the pulpit, and you are so good at it."

"Sure, older adult," Nadia said. "Happy to have your sermons benefit from my workouts at CrossFit."

Wait. You say that my story last Sunday about the little boy needing a dollar wasn't something that could have happened to me because I've never even been to Buffalo? Oh well. Next time I use that story, I'll give proper attribution: "Here's what the Lord would have done in Buffalo on a snowy Sunday morning if Betty Achtemier had taken me with her to Buffalo…"

Jim Wallis and Tony Campolo met with Bill Clinton years ago to help him repent. The only reason I wasn't there was I wasn't asked. I'm sure it was an oversight. Desperate for a good contrition story for a Maundy Thursday sermon, I thought it only right for me to say what I would have said if Bill had been smart enough to invite me. "So, like I said to Bill, 'Bill, old buddy, you can't…'" They loved it.

Footnotes are impossible in sermons and attribution ("As I read in a recent book by the Right Reverend Bishop N. T. Wright last week…") can come across as pompous and presumptuous. Though occasionally I will give credit by saying to the congregation, "All you bean counters, don't bother to google this story to find its true origin. It's from an April 1990 sermon by Fred Craddock. I recount Fred's story today as if it were my own as my humble homage to a great preacher."

Some years ago, somebody published a collection of women's sermons. After a long preface that argued forcefully that women preach in a way that is quite special, very perceptive, even unavailable to men, the book's first sermon was one that a woman on the West Coast had purloined from me! A sermon on John 3 that I had preached a few years before at Duke Chapel. Should I be flattered or incensed? When I complained to Stanley Hauerwas, he replied, "By God, you *do* preach like a woman! Besides, you've got too long an incriminating paper trail to be indignant that a fellow preacher snitched from you."

I know it's good to take sermon illustrations from your own life, but let's face it: my life hasn't been that interesting. People make way too much out of creativity and personal insight. I'm always grateful when, in the middle of my sermon preparation on a tough text, I stumble across a fellow preacher who can help me lift the luggage. If a preacher is vain enough to put stuff out on the web or to publish it, it's fair game. If I pay $19.95 for a book of your sermons, they're mine.

So, go ahead, all you possessive, miserly preachers. Lock it down, smack a © on it. You won't keep this professional purloiner from poaching your preachments (Matt 24:43). In the dead of night some Saturday, I'll creep in with a ski mask, crowbar, and flashlight, take your precious metaphor, and make it my own.

The ski mask and flashlight I stole from a speech by poet Billy Collins.

Journal for Preachers, Summer 2019

7

Powerful Preacher

Doing my bit in a voter registration drive while I was in college, I was in a little Southern town when the racially segregated schools were integrated. There was a meeting (attended only by people of my color) at the town's high school. What was to be done to "save our schools"? What could we do to keep "them" out of "our" schools? One by one, angry speakers rose to call for boycott, resistance, even force, whatever was necessary to protect "ours" from "theirs."

There was an old, half-broken Baptist preacher in that town who had baptized, married, or buried just about everyone at one time or another. His once-clear bass voice was now cracked, sign that he was about ready to be put out to pasture. He came late to the meeting that night. Stood at the back and silently listened.

After a half hour or so of the crowd's racist tirades, he half raised his hand to ask for the microphone. The crowd made way for their beloved pastor as he, with dignity and some ceremony, made his way to the podium. He stood before the microphone. Silently, his eyes slowly swept across the gathered throng in silence, then he spoke in measured, sure, certain cadence: "There is neither male nor female, Jew nor Greek, slave nor free, white nor black, rich or poor, educated or uneducated, for there is one Lord, one faith, one baptism. Go home, read your Bibles!"

He paused for effect. Then he slowly, dolorously said, "Looking over this assembly, gazing at your faces, I this night have realized that I am the worst preacher in the world."

A gasp from the gathered throng.

"If you think that anything in our faith justifies your presence here, that the sentiments expressed here tonight are in any way exemplary of the way of Christ, then I have failed miserably in my work as a preacher. I have poured out my life for nothing. Vanity, all is vanity. It's in the Bible."

Then, with the meeting reduced to stunned, awed silence, he ceremoniously walked to the back of the room and slammed the door as he left.

The presider made an awkward effort to resume the meeting, but for all intents and purposes the evening had ended. Slowly, people drifted out.

The schools integrated that fall without incident.

And I, college sophomore that I was, sat there stewing in my low, undergraduate imagination, muttering, "One day I'll have that much power. Go ahead, Lord, live dangerously, walk on the wild side; make me a preacher."

8
Powerful Prayer

A favorite student of mine was struck down with a brain tumor. I went over to Duke Hospital the night before his surgery. There were his parents, and his young wife (they had only been married a year). They all stood around his bedside, trying to be cheerful, but, like me, deeply fearful.

Eventually the neurosurgeon came by. He explained what he planned to do the next morning. "We'll slice open your skull here and open this up, and we'll work right in here and then we'll send it to pathology."

When he finished describing the gruesome procedure, he asked if there were any questions. We had none. The neurosurgeon then said, "Look, before I leave, would you like to have prayer?"

And we said, "Sure. In fact, you have two Methodist preachers right here."

The surgeon said he would lead the prayer. He asked that we all join hands around the bedside. Then he led one of the most powerful prayers I had ever heard in the hospital.

"First, I am going to pray for Clark, as we go into the surgery, that God's presence be with us. Then I am going to pray for me, that God will use my skills tomorrow, and then I will pray for you."

When he finished, there was not a dry eye around the bedside. It was powerful.

"Well," he said, "I've got to go."

I shot out of the door and went down the hall, calling after him. I told him I was a chaplain here and I said, "Wow. That was one of the most wonderful power prayers that I've ever heard. Do you offer that to everyone? I just think that was wonderful."

"Do you?" he asked. "I'm just not sure."

"Well, I know what you mean. This is a secular university with government regulations and everything. And you don't want to offend anyone," I said.

"That's not what I meant," he said. "You are a preacher. You know what it is like. You get into these situations in life, you invite Jesus in, you turn it over to the Lord. You just never know what Jesus is going to ask you to do. Do you?"

"Jesus's Health Care Plan," sermon,
Montreat, NC, 2009

9
Disorganized

My last Sunday at Duke Chapel was wonderful. A packed house. Full orchestra to back up the hundred-voice choir. Dozens of people in tears. In the recessional, babies held up before me for my blessing.

At least, that's how I remember it.

After service, as soon as the adoring, grateful throng had hugged me, thanked me, and dispersed, a student—a sophomore—came up to me and said, "I'm pissed at you. What am I going to do for spiritual guidance now?"

"I'm sure I'll be followed by some wonderful pastor," I said. "You'll get over me."

"Say," he continued, "will you be doing much preaching in your new job?"

"Of course," I responded. "As bishop I'll be preaching at least once every Sunday."

"Good," he said.

"Why 'good'?" I asked.

"Well, if you are going to be doing a lot of preaching, maybe now you can work on your organization. I had heard your sermons were hard to follow and that your brain didn't work like others," he said.

"Who said that about my preaching?" I asked with indignation.

"Well, *everybody*," he laughed. "If we can't follow you, do you really think people in Alabama can?"

"Look, kid," I said. "Are you open to accompanying me to Alabama to whisper the truth to me once a day? The church has given me a job where I can hurt people. So, I'll be surrounded by people who are too intimidated and who care too little about me to be truthful. If you could go with me, maybe I could become a great preacher."

Accidental Preacher: A Memoir, William
B. Eerdmans Publishing Company, 2019

10

So, You Want to Preach?

Dear Dr. Willimon:

Someday I would like to preach like you. I like your style. Could you advise me on which preparation would be best?

(Name withheld by request)

So, you want to preach?

Good.

Be birthed by a mother who, like old Hannah,
uses you as a bargaining chip with God,
promising to give you to God right after she's done with you.
Or be abandoned by your mother (or even better, father),
left as an orphan so frail you must run to God for safekeeping.
(Either way will do.)
So, you want to preach?
Have a storm-tossed, tormented youth.
Burn with passion's fires, satiate your desires. Or be the all-American boy,
President of the church youth group, Eagle in your Scout troop,
Model of morality for all teens less chaste to admire.
(Later, some congregation will feed like hogs on all your pent-up, unused desire.)

So, you want to preach?

Fall in love with words.
Collect clichés and burn them.
Imitate every well-wrought phrase you hear. Like Francis, exhort the birds.
Read all the plays (sonnets too) of Shakespeare.
(Anyone who despised God that much—and so eloquently, too—must be of interest to a would-be word peddler like you.)

So, you want to preach?

Poach from the poems of Yeats, consume the short stories of O'Connor.
Crib Augustine's *Confessions*. Swipe Schweitzer's *Quest*.
Steal the opinions of others before attempting any of your own.

This way, time-honored, is best.

Oh, yes, the novels of Walker Percy, the entire *Sunday Times.*

But never, never bother with anthologies of religious rhymes.

So, you want to preach?

Fall in love, and out again.

Be in pain.

Get lost.

Roam. Come back home.

Get saved.

In sin, be bold.

Walk out past the streetlights;

sit alone long nights in the cold

So, you want to preach?

Good.

Nothing bad ever happened to a preacher;

Wednesday's tragedy is fodder for Sunday's sermon.

A marital separation can be useful, or an unsuccessful operation.

Stare at yourself naked in the mirror;

Gape at your people when doing visitation.

Listen to their lives, their lies, their dreams, their hopes.

Keep notes.

Listen.

The things in life that hammer, wrack, and confuse—

these a homiletician knows how to use.

So, you want to preach?

Attend one of our first-rate theology schools.

Read all the required texts;

make friends with God's fools.

Increase your vocabulary of swollen words that end in *-tion.*

Half of this will be worthless, dated, scarcely ten years into your ministry.

What's not will preserve you from theological insanity.

So, you want to preach?

The Last Word: Insights About the Church and Ministry, Abingdon Press, 2000

11

My Encounter with a Chainsaw

This past Christmas, I wished for and received a chainsaw. On New Year's Eve, while I was engaged in a woodworking project, the chainsaw slipped, grabbed my left sleeve, threw me to the ground, and in a matter of seconds dug into my arm, cutting my hand and wrist to the bone for about six inches. I began bleeding profusely. My arm looked like a piece of fresh, badly butchered flank steak.

As my wife, Patsy, raced me to the emergency room, I considered the possibility that I would bleed to death. I was hoping that if the *Christian Century*'s editors considered me obituary-worthy, they might lie: "Bishop Willimon, a dedicated foe of injustice, was injured while cutting firewood for the poor." The truth: Using a tool for which I have no training or talent, I injured myself while attempting to carve a wooden salad bowl. I consoled myself with the thought that if I survived, I'd have something to share with friends in retirement at the Methodist Home. A chainsaw gash trumps a broken hip.

To my relief, chainsaw injuries are just another day at the office in the Sylva, North Carolina, emergency room. In no time I was lying on a gurney and receiving shots of morphine from the same nurse who had earlier chided me: "Hold that bandage tight, Buddy, and stop dripping blood on my floor."

I was soon on the mend, but not till after a couple of hours of surgery and a couple of days of agony. Cast out of the hospital into a cheap motel room, no morphine to comfort me, I reminded God of all the favors I had done for the Trinity. As I tossed and turned I considered the possibility that my accident was God's payback for all the lousy sermons that I've preached. I repented for any hubris that may have contributed to my scathing review of a book by Bart Ehrman (in the December 30 *Century*). I warned God that if some of the pain in my hand wasn't gone by morning, I would withdraw from the United Methodist Council of Bishops. I tried to think pleasant thoughts, but all I could think about was the scene in Mel Gibson's passion movie in which Jesus's hand is nailed to the cross.

It's humbling to learn firsthand how rapidly a mature, well-informed theology reverts to infantile bargaining, pleading and threats. Now in a long-term relationship with a physical therapist, I've reached a thank-God-it's-over frame of mind—but not before a bit of theological reflection. My thought is spurred by a question put to me by a layperson: "I suppose your accident caused you to do a lot of praying?"

Not really. I did a fair amount of cursing my stupidity during my nights in hell, but I offered few petitions to heaven. It's not that I lack faith in God's ability to heal. Scripture repeatedly shows that God heals. The advent of the reign of God is accompanied by Jesus doing many healings and exorcisms. Paul certainly thought of healing as a sign of God's active grace, and the Acts of the Apostles shows that Christ's healing continues through Christ's people, the church. Then there's James 5:13-16:

> Are any among you suffering? They should pray... They should call for the elders of the church and have them pray over them, anointing them with oil in the name of the Lord. The prayer of faith will save the sick... Pray for one another, so that you may be healed. (NRSV)

Although Luther didn't think much of the letter of James, John Wesley loved it. I believe that prayer can heal, and I've witnessed miraculous healings in my own pastorates. So why was I, cast into extremis by a chainsaw, reluctant to pray?

For one thing, I hoped that God would be busy with the mess in the Middle East and wouldn't find out about the mess I had made of myself with a chainsaw. After my stunt, the boss would be fully justified in demanding my clerical credentials, adding, "An idiot like you has no business caring for any church."

More important is my sense that this passage from James has, in our hands, done much mischief. In many of the churches I visit on Sundays, it is the custom for the pastor, at some point in the service, to ask, "Are there any prayer requests?" Then cometh the reading of the sick list, mostly a tale of woe about the physical deterioration of the congregation's senior citizens. There may be pain, injustice and the ravages of nature elsewhere, but for us, the purpose of prayer is purely physical—and it's all about us.

A sign in front of one congregation proclaimed it as "The Place for People in Pain." My heart went out to the pastor: if these people are anything like me, being in pain makes them, well, a pain. "Forty Days of Recovery," said another church sign. Are you talking about Lent? I don't think we ever actually recovered from that illness. I was even in a congregation where the bulletin included two pages of "prayer concerns" with the sufferers categorized by their particular ailments.

This is not prayer as Jesus practiced and taught it. Bread and debts are mentioned in the Lord's Prayer, but infection and discomfort are not. Prayer in Jesus's name is noted for his demand that we pray for our enemies, not our illnesses. I've recently heard prayers about radical mastectomies, testicular tumors and sprained index fingers but can't tell you when I've heard a really good intercession for Osama bin Laden.

We've given ourselves over completely to obsession with physical health. People who otherwise never see their pastors do see them when they're sick. Sickness has become the most interesting thing that happens to us, that which gives our lives significance—and prayer is a remedy of last resort when other methods of treatment have failed. God, though lacking credentials, is reduced to being a member of the health-care-delivery team.

So before you pray, consider the sort of God whom you address and the possible cost of asking this God, "How then shall I live, now that I'm sick?" Prayer "in Jesus's name" is a risk. Bring God into a situation and you don't know where God will take things. I have known many who earnestly implored God to come into their lives, take away their pain and heal them of their infirmities—only to have God refuse. It was as if Jesus put them in worse discomfort than their illness itself by coming to them not with, "There, there, everything's going to be all right," but rather with a hearty, "Follow me!" They prayed for palliation and got instead another assignment. Only Jesus would turn a person's pain into an occasion for vocation.

Prayer is more than my bringing my wish list to Jesus, asking him for occasional help with the heavy lifting. Prayer is also the risky attempt to let Jesus speak. So to be honest, I didn't pray when I was in pain because the last thing I wanted to do was risk a visit by Jesus, which might make my life even more difficult than it was at that moment. I wanted to be pain-free, and I wanted healing now—no matter what Jesus had in mind.

I avoided saying much to God about my accident while I was down and out. But God did take the opportunity to say some things to me. Before my brush with a chainsaw, I was suspicious of claims for the pedagogical uses of pain. I now know better. For one thing, I couldn't get out of my head the sight of my body, reduced to red meat and spouting blood. Genesis 3:19b, on our destiny in dirt, sprang immediately to mind. Sometimes the truth that our faith has to teach can come only through a revealing God who is willing to speak even through a chainsaw to make a point.

In pain, rendered dependent in an instant (I couldn't even open a medicine bottle without help) and not in the best of moods, I rediscovered the gift of hospitality in others' welcoming hands: strangers in the emergency room, my doctor (whose first words to me were not "How can I fix you up?" but rather, "Let me first say how sorry I am that this happened to you"), my patient wife and attentive children and church friends. I've always preached the Christian faith as training in the art of dependency—experience of the divine through the hands of strangers—but sometimes

God doesn't begin the remedial tutorial until we are on our knees. Though I wouldn't for anything repeat the misery of the past months, I'm much better at practicing the faith that earlier I only professed.

In my agony, I thought, This too shall pass. I'll probably make it through this and one day have difficulty even remembering how bad I'm hurting now. Though I was in that heightened narcissistic state that often afflicts people in pain, God got through to me, reminding me of all those suffering souls for whom pain is chronic, to whom even the coming of the dawn brings no help. That many of them can go on with dignity—worshiping God, caring about someone other than themselves, laughing at a joke, holding themselves accountable to discipleship—is one of the great mysteries of our faith, a testimonial to the God who works the nightshift. As Jesus said of his friend Lazarus's terminal illness, even this can be "for God's glory."

Paul said that the occasionally awful suffering of this present age can't separate us from the love of God in Christ. Paul was right. In spite of my utterly self-centered agony, I found myself thinking about my neighbors who don't have health insurance. My recovery is going to cost around $10,000, but I'll barely feel that pain.

Praise be to the God who uses even our worst screw-ups to instill in us empathy that we could never have on our own. We who worship God on a cross ought to know how to expect more of our times of illness. There was a day when health didn't mean just freedom from pain and physical soundness—it also meant wholeness, even holiness. For Christians, healing, as a gift of God, is always subservient to the gifts of fidelity and discipleship.

In the end I did pray, bypassing petition and heading straight to thanksgiving. I thanked God for my doctors and my anesthesiologist. I offered a special doxology for that nurse with the morphine. I also thanked God for the visceral, attention-getting reminder of my mortality and for my state of blessed, never-ending dependency that's sometimes obscured by the delusions engendered by transitory good health.

I preached on a recent Sunday, gesticulating in the air with my plastic splint for 20 minutes. After the service, a kid with purple hair came up to me and asked the question that no one else had the nerve to ask.

"What'd you do to your arm? Carpal tunnel syndrome?"

"No, this is a real man's injury," I responded. "A chainsaw did this to me."

"Bummer, man," said the kid. "You're just like me."

"How do you mean?" I asked.

"I did a stupid thing too," he confided. "Busted my butt on my skateboard. Cracked my elbow. It hurt like hell—couldn't skate for two months. My friends made fun of me. Still hurts. Just like you, I said to Jesus, 'Get me out of this and I'll never skate again.'"

"Did you keep your promise to Jesus?" I asked my younger brother in Christ.

"Naw," he said, "all I learned was next time to be more careful about making any promises to Jesus!"

"Yep," I replied. "I learned a lot too."

The Christian Century, April 21, 2009

Part Two

Seeds

A farmer went out to scatter seed...
Some fell on the path...
Other seed fell on rocky ground...
Other seed fell among thorny plants...
Other seed fell on good soil...

Matthew 13:3-8

12

Tough Way to Make a Living

Working with words is hard.

See? That's not the best way to begin, but it was all I could come up with. Miss McDaniel taught me always to begin with a topical sentence "which encapsulates, in no more than ten words, everything you intend to say in the essay." But in her sixth-grade class, we were always writing about easy subjects like "The Future of My Country." Here it's different. Try to say something on a really important subject, and watch the right words duck for cover. So, all I can think to say is, I hate words.

That's the thing about words. You can't buy the right one when you need it. When you don't need words—say, when you're supposed to be quietly, empathetically listening to a parishioner—your words ooze out over everything, nervously filling all the empty spaces. You can't stop talking. But Saturday night, after a tough week—pulpit waiting for you like a hangman's rope in a few hours, you staring at a blank sheet of paper—where are the words?

Words are as common as dirt at the gym when you are trying to work out and avoid the retired guys who insist on chatting you up or on television or during a presidential campaign, but before a couple of parents whose four-year-old child has just died of cancer, you can't get a good word for love or money.

Augustine referred derisively to the role of "word Merchant." That's us on Sundays. All we've got to offer, the only thing standing between us and God, is words. There are gods who get close to people through war, or sex, or nature. Unfortunately for us preachers, our God, the God of Israel and the church, loves words. If we want to get to this God, it's through words or not at all. God speaks and the world springs into being (*ex nihilo*). I can't even get a decent sermon when I need it on Sunday. It's a tough way to make a living.

As for me, I like to be in control. I don't expect to be brilliant, just to know where all of this is going to end by noon. Yet these words keep slipping from my grasp, jumping the tracks, getting lost in the congregation, whooping it up, running naked down the aisles.

I tell myself, "After all, this is *my* sermon." Then, scarcely have the words left my mouth (you can see it on people's faces as they sit and listen) when my words have been adopted, purloined as *their* words. They're not even waiting for the sermon to be over. Already they are working on sermons of their own, taking over words that were first mine. You can't keep words in their place.

So, they say, at the front door of the church after the sermon, "That really was a great sermon about..."

And I listen, but I can't hear my sermon. It's no good to say, "You idiot! My sermon was not about that; it was about this."

Too late. The words are now running loose, frolicking about the congregation, stirring up all manner of mischief, dressing up in different clothes, strutting like they owned the place. Someday these let-loose words will come back to haunt you, make you wish you had never gone out in public with that word.

I put my words down on sheets of paper. *There, that ought to hold you*, I say. Even there, in print, they will not stay in place. Paper and print give the illusion of stability and permanence. I just threw away the dictionary that got me through college because so many of the words had changed definitions. And I'm not all that old.

No wonder someone is always misunderstanding, misconstruing my words. I say, "Well, what I meant to say was..." But it's no good. The words are gone, set loose. I asked an old preacher what had he learned in his fifty years in the pulpit and he replied, "The possibilities for being misunderstood are infinite."

A few years ago, I did a book on burnout among the clergy. I was surprised (why should I have been?) to hear, in my interviews with clergy, that one of the most debilitating, depressing aspects of pastoral work was preaching. Blame it on the words.

I learned how great a challenge it is to give oneself, week after week, to so fragile an art. We work, chiseling these sermons out of the hard granite of the biblical text. We speak. Our words bounce off the walls, ricochet off the ceiling, and then die, soaked up by the pew cushions, or else burrowed deep in people's brains, waiting for the proper time to hatch, to jump you from behind as they say, "A few weeks ago, didn't you say in a sermon...?"

I hate words. They're always changing hats, putting on airs, taking up residence at another address, mocking you, saying, "I don't mean that. I haven't meant that since late in the Bush administration. Now I mean..."

Words like *gay* or *girl* or *preacher* are too nimble on their feet. The other day, in a meeting, someone said that we needed to "*massage* this plan a little longer before it's ready."

Who invited a word like that into a meeting like this?

Some words grow limp with use, overuse. Once we could truly celebrate something. Then the church got hold of the word and preachers started celebrating this, celebrating that. When everything was a celebration, nothing was left to celebrate. Just the other day I saw *liberation*, *freedom*, and *community*—all words with a distinguished past—on their way out to the lexical cemetery. Now I'm forced to search for substitutes. Many perfectly good words refuse to work for clergy, probably because they've heard of how we've abused their relatives.

Otherwise respectable words, like *commitment*, *stewardship*, *witness*, and *evangelistic*, have now been transmogrified into a sort of sweet ooze. Use them on Sunday and watch the congregation's eyes glaze over. I hate the way words do that.

It's only four days until I've got to come up with something to say on Sunday. This is not a promising beginning. I'm groping. My mind has degenerated into an article from *Reader's Digest*. I have become a linguistic loser on *Wheel of Fortune*. Somebody get me Roget on the phone. I'm not even sure if I know what the word *means* means. The words are hiding. They wouldn't be seen dead in public with me. I'm sounding ridiculous. My readers' eyes are glazing over. A word, a word, my kingdom for one lousy word. Miss McDaniel is ashamed of me. I hate words. Unfortunately, the only cure for this or any other human malady is more words.

The Last Word: Insights About the
Church and Ministry, Abingdon Press, 2000

13
Death in North Carolina

All Saints afternoon, Durham, North Carolina. A group of Duke students cavorted on the lawn in front of the chapel with helium-filled balloons. The sky was clear; it was unseasonably warm—a perfect day for a fall picnic. Campus Ministry had organized an All Saints gathering in front of the chapel. As the carillon pealed "Sine Nomine," someone sang solo, "For All the Saints." Multicolored balloons, each imprinted with a favorite saint's name, were released to the heavens, one by one, as people shouted, "Saint Francis," "Saint Joan of Arc," "Saint Nicholas." The balloons drifted up, borne eastward toward Raleigh by a gentle afternoon breeze.

Later that evening, a cold front moved through North Carolina. Some of those same students shivered in darkness before the gates of

Central Prison, keeping vigil. At 2 a.m., Margie Velma Barfield became the first woman to be executed in North Carolina in forty years.

"Isn't this typical of Christians?" one person commented. "A woman is poisoned to death by the government, and we are playing with balloons." What would he suggest Christians do? I wondered. Many of us had hoped that politically moderate governor Jim Hunt might stay Velma's execution. Hunt, who at the time was locked in an ugly battle to unseat ultraconservative senator Jesse Helms, rejected Barfield's pleas. (Why is it that we keep thinking that it really makes a difference whether or not a liberal is in the White House? As Governor Hunt demonstrated, when the chips are down, the difference between one Caesar and another is mainly a matter of style. Helms won anyway.)

Perhaps the most disarming aspect of the Barfield execution was that she was a Christian herself. Those of us who oppose the death penalty have been caught in a bind more than once when the person to be executed happened to be a child molester or a mass murderer. The Barfield case, however, pushed advocates of capital punishment to the wall in defense of their position. Would they now say that this woman should die?

The fifty-two-year-old grandmother was a lifelong fundamentalist Baptist and Sunday school teacher who broke stereotypes of murderers. At her trial she never denied killing her boyfriend by lacing his beer and tea with arsenic before they left for church one evening. She said that she was insane at the time, still coping with the horrors of her deprived and abusive childhood and hooked on a variety of drugs. The poison was only meant to make him sick, she said, so that he wouldn't discover that she had been signing his name to checks.

People in her community earlier had praised Barfield for getting her boyfriend to go to church and for reducing his heavy drinking. Later she confessed to poisoning three other people, one a preacher like me, but she was tried and convicted only for her boyfriend's death.

"I tell you, Velma is a changed woman. She's been born again," pleaded her red-faced, fundamentalist pastor, as he spoke of her recent religious experience while in jail. "She's a child of God."

Local right-wing evangelicals—who stress the power of life-changing, instantaneous conversion experiences—were at some pains to explain why Barfield's conversion did not really change anything about Velma. Yet her little preacher stood beside her to the end.

On her last day on this earth, Barfield read her Bible and religious pamphlets. And she listened to a tape that Mrs. Billy Graham had sent her. After directing that all her usable organs be donated for transplant, she said that she hoped her death could allow victims' families to piece their lives back together. She then said that she did not fear death, because she had put her trust in the Lord.

That evening she ate her last meal—a Coke and a package of Cheez Doodles from the prison canteen. She put on her pink cotton pajamas and walked to the room where she was executed by lethal injection.

A sixteen-year-old student, Laura Miller, stood outside the prison gates holding a sign reading, "THOSE WITHOUT THE CAPITAL GET THE PUNISHMENT." The little group keeping vigil stood for a few more minutes in the dark and embraced one another. Some wept. Then they disappeared into the night.

Yet even in the midnight, clouded skies, some saw it: a bright green balloon—floating gently skyward over the sleeping city, alone, yet drawn toward some distant place, tugged by an irresistible force—imprinted with the name Margie Velma.

The Christian Century,
November 28, 1984

14

Father's Day

This summer, we drove down to somewhere between Lake City and Coward, South Carolina (do you know the place?) to hear my father-in-law preach his (third) farewell sermon as he prepared to retire (for the third time) from the Christian ministry After his first retirement, ten years ago, he was sent to tiny rural churches where no one else would go. But this year he told them that now, at last, he was going to retire for good and move to the mountains of Hendersonville, North Carolina, to live among the Floridians.

The hot Sunday sun rose over green tobacco fields as the service began in the little church. He had asked a quartet of sweet, soprano voices to sing his favorite, "The Ninety-and-Nine." You remember, it's a song about the Lost Sheep: "There were ninety-and-nine, safe in the fold..." I don't think I'd heard it since I was a child. Don't think it's ever been sung in Duke Chapel.

After they sang, he preached. Before he set off for the mountains and Hendersonville, Carl Parker preached. His text? Something from Paul about the depth and breadth, the height and width of the love of God. It was Father's Day, so he talked a little bit about how we fathers all love and cherish our children. God loves us even more than that, he said.

Then he spoke about the man who was to die in the electric chair in South Carolina the next day. I had seen his picture on the news the night before. Somebody had held a service of remembrance for this man's victims and their families. He had killed a couple of people, maimed others, in his rampage of terror. The preacher at *that* service had declared that he wished they would let him "throw the switch on this piece of refuse who destroyed these innocent lives." Mr. Parker went into lurid detail describing the crimes of this man.

"And yet," he said, "today's scripture, as well as the sweet song we have heard, says that God loves that man on death row, values his soul just as much as God values us."

The congregation got real quiet.

"Why, according to Jesus's story of the Lost Sheep, God will gladly leave us ninety-and-nine gathered in the fold here this morning and go to Columbia to death row just to get hold of that one lost sheep. And when God finds him, God's happier to have him than to have all of us safe ones here in church."

I noted, at the end of the service, that congregation seemed much more willing to let Preacher Parker go on and retire to Hendersonville. He is old, long past time for respectable retirement. They've got him now safely stored among the Floridians in Hendersonville. You're safe. He won't be preaching too much anymore.

"The Unfettered Word," sermon, Duke
University Chapel, October 15, 1989

15

What I'm Trying to Say Is...

My colleague Richard Lischer plans to give the students in his introductory preaching classes a list of stories and illustrations that have collapsed into clichés because preachers have used them too often. That's the trouble with us preachers. When we find a good story or perfect illustration, we steal it back and forth from one another and use, reuse, and overuse it until it goes limp.

Once, we had three successive guest preachers in the Duke University Chapel end their sermons with the story of the boy on the gallows from Elie Wiesel's novel *Night*. It's a moving, evocative, and powerful story, but it had lost its punch by the third telling. If we preachers can enervate so powerful a story, how much less effective do we make our weaker illustrations?

A myriad of once-good stories need to die a dignified death. Among the candidates for narrative euthanasia:

➤   "He ain't heavy; he's my brother"

➤   "Christ has no hands but our hands"

➤   Frederick Buechner's vision of a departed friend

➤   Will Campbell's story of the Easter chicken

➤   Reynolds Price's baptism dream story

Use any of these and watch the congregation's eyes glaze over. Then there's the problem of stock words and phrases. We tend to dip into this bargain basement when things aren't going well in the sermon, when we are groping for what to say next or buying time until we can remember our second point:

➤   Today I'd like you to consider...

➤   Some of you are saying to yourselves that this text is [fill in the blank: irrelevant; weird; not in the Bible; not worth a sermon], but I say to you that [in twenty minutes I can show you why it's important; it's in the lectionary, so who are you to say?; Jesus didn't really mean this the way it sounds]...

➤   Moving right along...

➤   Back to today's assigned text...

➤   One time there was a [little boy; little girl; squirrel]...

➤   Many of you are saying to yourselves...

➤   In conclusion...

➤   Finally...

➤ One last, quick comment...

➤ If time permitted...

➤ Maybe next Sunday I'll be able to explain...

➤ Well, you see what I'm driving at is...

➤ Finally, let us pray...

➤ Just the other day my nine-year-old niece said to me...

➤ It's perhaps best summed up in the words of [the old hymn; the poem by Robert Frost; that witty saying by Winston Churchill, something I think Gandhi once said, or maybe it was Douglas MacArthur]...

➤ Again, let me reiterate...

We preachers not only bring our people close to God, we also protect them from God—often without knowing that we're doing so. One way we keep them safe from divine incursion is by talking about holy things in a way that devalues them. Therefore, one essential homiletical discipline is custody of the tongue, vigilance against creeping cliché. Talk about God ought not to be cheap.

The Last Word: Insights About the
Church and Ministry, Abingdon Press, 2000

16
Sent

At age ten, I was doing time in Miss McDaniel's sixth-grade class, dutifully copying inanities off the blackboard, when I got the call. A note was delivered by one of the toadies from the front office. Old Lady McDaniel read the note and then called out, "Willimon. Mr. Harrelson" (the intimidating, iron-fisted, ancient principal) "wants to see you."

With trepidation, I lifted my desktop, put away my things, and trudged toward the principal's office. As I passed an open door, a classmate looked out with pity, praying, *Thank God it's him and not me.* Ascending the gallows, I went over in my mind all the possible misunderstandings that could have led to this portentous subpoena. *I was only a distant witness to the rock-through-the-gym-window incident, in no way a perpetrator or even passive conspirator.*

"Listen carefully. I do not intend to repeat myself," said the principal, looking down at me. "You, go down Tindal two blocks and turn left, go two more blocks, number 15. I've got a message to be delivered. You tell Jimmy Spain's mother if he's not in school by this afternoon, I'm reporting her for truancy."

So, this wasn't about me. It was worse. *God help me. Jimmy Spain, toughest thug of all the sixth grade.* If we lived in a just world, Jimmy should have been in the eighth. *And what in God's name is "truancy"?*

Somber thoughts tormented me as I journeyed down Tindal, bidding farewell to the safety of the schoolyard, turned left, walked two more blocks, marveling that the world actually went about its business while we did time in school.

Under a darkening sky, the last two blocks descended into a not-nice part of town unknown to me or any of my friends, a sad neighborhood that hid behind the school. Number 15 was a small house, peeling paint, bare yard—just the sort of house you'd expect Jimmy Spain to be holed up in, rough, sinister. A reassuring blue Buick was parked in front. As I fearfully approached the walk, a man emerged, letting the screen door slam as he stepped off the porch, adjusted his tie, stretched his suspenders, and lit a cigar.

"Are you, Mr. . . . Spain, sir?" As the words came out of my mouth, I remembered that everybody at school said that Jimmy was so mean because he didn't have a daddy.

The man looked down at me, pulled taut his tie, and guffawed. "Mr. Spain?" Haw, haw, haw. "Mr. Spain, my ass."

He sent up a cloud of smoke, pushed himself into his Buick, and sped off. (Not until the eighth grade did someone whisper the word for what Jimmy's mother did for a living. At the Boy Scout Court of Honor I saw again the man who had brushed me aside. A member of city council, he pinned on my First Class Scout Badge.)

I stepped on the rotten porch and tapped the soiled screen door. My heart sank. The door was opened by none other than Jimmy Spain. His reptilian green eyes enlarged when he saw me, startled as much by me as I was by him. Before Jimmy could say anything, the door was pulled back and a woman in a faded blue terrycloth bathrobe inspected me, looking over Jimmy's shoulder.

"What do you want?" she asked. A mother smoking, and in a bathrobe, even though it's midday?

"Er, I'm from the school. The principal sent me, to, uh . . ."

"Principal! What does that old fool want?"

"Er, he sent me to say that we, er, that is, that everybody at school, that we all miss Jimmy and wish he were there today."

"What?" she sneered, pulling Jimmy toward her.

"It's like a special day and everyone wants Jimmy there. We are doing some special stuff. Music maybe. Ice cream, for all I know. Everybody thinks it won't be as special if Jimmy's not there. At least, I think that's what he said."

Jimmy—the thug who could beat up any kid at Donaldson Elementary, even ninth graders, anytime he wanted—Jimmy peered out at me in . . . wonderment. Suddenly this hood, feared by all, looked small, being clutched by his mother, his eyes embarrassed, hanging on my every stammering word.

"You tell that old man it's none of his damn business what I do with James. James," she said, looking down at him (*"James"?*), "you want to go to that stupid school today or not?"

Jimmy didn't take his eyes off me as he wordlessly nodded assent.

"Suit yourself. Get your stuff. And take that dollar off the dresser to buy lunch. I ain't got nothing here."

In a flash he was away and back. His mother stood at the door and stared suspiciously, and after giving Jimmy an unimaginable peck on the cheek, watched as we walked off the rotting porch, down the walk, and back toward Tindal Avenue. We said not a word. I had previously lacked the courage to speak to Jimmy the Hood, and Jimmy the Tough had never had any reason, thank the Lord, to speak to me. Walking back to school that afternoon was no time to begin.

I think we didn't talk because each of us knew, without knowing, that we had been part of something bigger than us, more than words could say.

We walked up the steps to the school, took a right, and wordlessly turned toward the principal's office. Jimmy allowed himself to be led by me. I handed him off to the principal's secretary. For the first time Jimmy seemed not mean and threatening but small. As the secretary led him away, Jimmy turned and looked back with a look of... I don't know, maybe regret, embarrassment? But it could have also been thanks, gratitude.

That evening, when I narrated my day to my mother at supper of minute steak and mashed potatoes, she exclaimed, "That is the most outrageous thing I've ever heard! Sending a young child out in the middle of the school day to fetch a truant. And on that street! Mr. Harrelson ought to have his head examined. Don't you ever allow anyone again to put you in that position. Sending a child!"

My mother was wrong. That day was my best at Donaldson Elementary. That day explained everything, preparation for the rest of my accidental life, my first comedic brush with a God who thinks nothing of commandeering ordinary boys and handing them outrageous assignments.

I didn't know then, but that day, on Tindal Avenue, old man Harrelson conducted a dress rehearsal for a midsummer night two decades later when I knelt before a bishop who laid on hands and said, "You, go down Tindal two blocks and turn left. God has a message to be delivered."

Accidental Preacher: A Memoir, William
B. Erdmans Publishing Company, 2019

17
The Gospel in Seven Words

God refuses to be God without us.

18
Sermon Slips

A deep, irrational fear grips every preacher—the fear of inadvertently saying something inappropriate, tasteless, suggestive, or just plain stupid while preaching. Preachers have been known to wake up screaming in the middle of the night, haunted by nightmares of saying something that doesn't come out the way they intend, in front of five hundred people. A slip of the tongue in the middle of a sermon is called "Freudian" by some, evidence of the humility-producing power of the Holy Spirit by others.

Once you've said it, there is no way to get out of a sermonic slip, no matter how hard you try. You can't go back and explain. It is best to have the congregation immediately stand for the benediction.

I was preaching in a large auditorium in the West. Jet lag had taken its toll—at least that's my best excuse. The person who introduced me had told the crowd of students that I was a great preacher, much in demand, interesting, controversial, and expensive.

The pressure was on.

I launched into my sermon, a simple piece unworthy of such an extravagant introduction. "When the sermon is weak, say it louder," somebody once told me. So, I was loud, emotional, passionate.

"And what is the most significant event our faith has to offer?" I asked. "The erection!" I bellowed.

Someone in the front row screamed.

"I mean the *resurrection!*" I said the correct word at least twelve more times. Didn't seem to do any good. Church was out.

"I'm sure I shall remember your sermon for the rest of my life," a young woman told me after the service. I could hear her guffawing as she walked out of the building and down the street.

On another occasion, I was speaking in the Midwest. I spoke mightily, and at length, perhaps being too attentive to how I was speaking rather than to what I was saying. Afterward, as we left the auditorium, I hesitantly asked my host—who could be intimidating—"Well, how do you think it went?"

"Rather well," he said. I sighed in relief. "Except for a couple of small matters," he continued. "Jesus was born in Bethlehem, not Jerusalem. Matthew was a tax collector, not a Pharisee. And the capital of Iowa is Des Moines, not Cedar Rapids."

Picky, picky, picky.

A distinguished yet insufferably pompous evangelist was preaching before a gathering of Presbyterian ministers. He was attacking moral decadence, particularly sexual sin in contemporary society, which is risky business for a preacher prone to sermonic slips.

"I remember," he shouted, "when we looked up to women, expected them to set the moral tone for society. We placed them on a pedestal. But not anymore. Have you seen the scandalous way women dress today?"

To illustrate his dubious point, he offered his former organist as an example. "Our organist, a precious young woman, came to practice for the service, dressed in a pair of short, tight, hiked-up running shorts. It was disgraceful! Walking into the Lord's house in those skimpy tight shorts. I determined to intervene. It was my duty as a pastor. I confronted her and asked her to come down to my study and talk about it. I shared Scripture with her and told her how those shorts looked. And I'll tell you, in fifteen minutes *I had those shorts off of her!*"

He tried to retrieve the hysterically hooting congregation, but his efforts were in vain. Each time he attempted to resume his sermon, some corner of the congregation would erupt into renewed laughter.

So, he asked them to stand for the execution, er, uh, I mean benediction.

The Christian Ministry,
November–December 1988

19

School

Remember what it's like to be in school? I'm old, grown-up, beyond the reach of public education, but I can still remember a little bit about school. For one thing, I remember the smell. Schools smell like...well, schools...they have a special odor. Not a bad odor exactly. It's just an odor like...school. I remember smelling a similar odor when I visited a parishioner in the state penitentiary. A coincidence? You make the call.

Another thing. When I was in school, they didn't have telephones. Back then, there was only one telephone. It was sequestered at the off-limits office. It's defended by this guard dog with glasses, the same one who protects the permission slips, staplers, and three-pronged adapter plugs. Even if you're a teacher, you have to go through this bouncer to use the telephone. In those days, schools believed that if you let in more telephones some geometry teacher might try to use it without permission, and the whole place would explode into anarchy. Once they got you in school, teacher or student, they don't want you trying to make contact with the real world.

Many of my fondest memories of school involve being sent by the teacher to go look for a three-pronged adapter plug for the filmstrip projector. The teacher would come in on Monday with a suspicious headache, look us over, groan, and say, "Class, today we're going to have a filmstrip on 'Rubber Cultivation in Borneo.'" Curtis Clinkscales would ask, "But isn't this a class in geometry?"

"Shut up, Curtis," she would explain.

She would get the film out of the can, have us move our desks back, struggle to get the screen hoisted, take the cord to the projector in hand, look at it, and say, "Oh God. Give me a break. Williamson, Williston, Willimon, whatever, go get the adapter plug."

The rest of the class hated me for it.

I'd go down the hall, down the steps, over to the principal's office to the guard dog stationed there. "No, you can't use the telephone," she would say before I could ask.

"We need a three-pronged plug," I'd say.

So, I was off to Drama, then by the band room, a quick stop at Social Studies, glancing briefly out the third-floor stairway window. "Look, there are people out there. Driving cars. Walking dogs." (It always comes as a shock, when you're languishing in school, that there are people running loose.) Fifteen gloriously wasted minutes later I give the news, "No adapter to be found, Miss Boggs."

"Sit down," she ordered. She then did the only thing a creative person in her desperate situation could do. She went to the door of the classroom, looked both ways up and down the hall to be sure the principal was nowhere to be seen, turned her back discreetly to the class, and then ripped that third prong off that plug, shoved that plug into the receptacle, and told us that this was our opportunity to know more about "Rubber Cultivation in Borneo" than anybody else in Greenville.

"Jesus Goes to School," sermon, Duke
University Chapel, December 22, 1991

20
Who's the King?

Sunday of Christ the King, in a desperate attempt to interest a disinterested congregation in the theological implications of the kingship of Christ, I cleverly began my sermon asking, "Do you need a king?" I admitted that they didn't think they wanted a king or queen since we are Americans, democratically disposed, averse to monarchy.

"But do you *need* a king? I'm not talking about some polo-playing playboy who dabbles in architecture," said I. "I'm talking about a real king. I'm not talking about a pleasant woman clutching a purse, wearing a small hat and sensible shoes. I'm talking about somebody to set things right, somebody who's in charge."

Then I went on to speak of the lordship, the kingship, of Christ and its implications.

After service, as people were shuffling past me on their way out, mumbling, "Nice sermon," a woman, husband in tow, approached— she was clutching a purse and wearing a small hat and sensible shoes. "Did it not occur to you that you might have British subjects in the congregation this morning?" she snorted.

"Oh, gosh, I guess we've even got people from Michigan," I said.

"You are not funny. In fact, you are extremely disgusting. Our queen is ten times the Christian of your silly actor president," she shouted, threatening me with her purse.

"Gosh, I would hate to put that to a vote here," I said jovially.

"You are not funny. You are silly. Juvenile. I intend to report you to your superiors!" A crowd was gathering, a number of students delighted to see this British visitor take the preacher apart. Being from South Carolina, I had no idea who my superiors were.

As she finally pulled her husband out the door, one of the students (you know who you are) muttered, "We broke away from those people for stuff like that." A comeback so wonderful, I wish I had thought of it myself.

"Who's in Charge Here?" sermon,
Duke University Chapel, November 22, 1992

21
Teach 'em a Lesson

There was a distinguished leader of business. He had built his company up from nothing to really something. He was chair of his church's board as well as the Chamber of Commerce. And Rotary. The church fellowship hall was named in honor of his generous gift.

Because he had worked so hard to build up his company, and because his leadership set the moral tone for the corporation, when he heard that a person in the accounting division had been pilfering, he said, "*Fire her!* Then turn it over to the cops. Teach her a lesson."

Sometime later, a teenager broke into the man's prized Mercedes coupe, went on a joy ride, and bashed the car into a fire hydrant. As an example to all the other wayward youth of the community, he said, "He's nineteen. Ought to know better. *Put him in the slammer.* It'll teach him a lesson."

When his son crashed out of his second drug treatment program since flunking out of college—an expensive one in New England—he said, "That's it. Had it with that boy. *Disinherit him.* It'll teach him a lesson."

In due time the man died. He went before his Maker. And when the man thought back on the way he had lived, all the times that he had come down hard on others, the deaf ear he had turned to their pleas for mercy, he trembled.

And from the great throne of heaven, the Judge of all looked down upon him and thundered, "*Forgive him!* It'll teach him a lesson."

22

In the Presence of a Prophet

One Sunday evening a fellow campus troublemaker barged in my dorm room in Shipp Hall, saying, "Give me a cigarette. Guess who I just sat across from on the flight from DC to Greenville/Spartanburg? Martin Luther Damn King! Just like he looks on TV. He slumped in his seat as soon as he got on the plane. Looked real tired. So I didn't bother him. Finally I got up the nerve to speak.

"'Dr. King, it's an honor to meet you. I'm active at my college, Wofford, in the movement. I'm coming from a training session in Washington. I really appreciate what you are doing.'"

"Unbelievable!" I exclaimed. "What did Dr. King say to you?"

"Nothing. So I said, 'Dr. King, my father is a farmer in low-country South Carolina. He's such a racist. I have tried to talk to him, tried to explain why the fight for racial justice is so important. But he says terrible things. I'm not going home for Thanksgiving because I don't want anything to do with such a redneck, racist old fool. His—'

"Dr. King lunged across the aisle, grabbed my arm, and said in a voice loud enough to wake the whole plane, 'You got to love your daddy!' Then he went back to sleep until we landed."

Accidental Preacher: A Memoir, William
B. Eerdmans Publishing Company, 2019

23
Successful Preaching

There I was, stuck with a testy text like Matthew 19:16-26: Jesus and the rich young man. Great. I'm supposed to stand up on the middle of a modem, elitist, secular, power-hungry university (is there any other kind?) and speak about Jesus causing a bad case of depression in an otherwise successful, upwardly mobile young adult? Give me a break.

In my sermon, I attempted to steer close to the text. This is a call story, I said. Someone is being summoned to follow Jesus. There's no way to sidestep that the story ends in despair. The young man's countenance falls, and Jesus notes the impossibility of saving the rich. As far as I can recall, this is the only call story in this Gospel where Jesus directly invites someone to discipleship and the person refuses. And the reason for the refusal? Money.

As I said, it's a tough text in my context.

So I preached it, restraining my inclination to explain away the culminating despair, trying hard not to tie it up with a bow. After all, Matthew just lets it hang there, so why shouldn't I?

The next morning, Monday, in the breakfast line in the university cafeteria, I encountered the chair of the department of religion. "Well, what happened yesterday?" he asked.

"Yesterday?" I asked.

"The sermon! Just couldn't think of an ending, could we? Sort of got it all out on the table but didn't know what to make of it, right?"

"Er, uh, right."

"Well, don't worry," he said. "You're usually quite adequate. Can't be good on every Sunday, can we?"

I staggered with my tray of grapefruit and Raisin Bran toward my table, but not before being intercepted by the dean of the divinity school.

"Did I sympathize with you in the service!" he said. "After that dull anthem, well, what hope was there for your sermon? There was no way for you to salvage things after that! You've got to demand that those musicians give you more help."

"Er, uh, right. That was what I was thinking."

I collapsed at the table, slumped over the Raisin Bran.

A young man, graduate student in forestry, came up to me. "That sermon," he said.

"Look, kid," I said, "I may have to take crap off of them, but I certainly don't have to take it off of you. Don't start on me about that sermon."

He looked confused (not a particularly unusual look for someone in forestry). Then he continued, "You know me—religious experience in college, gave my life to Christ. I thought Jesus was supposed to be nice! I know someone told me that. I just went home and cried."

"You *cried*?" I asked.

"Yep, just lay on my bed and wept. I asked Jesus, 'Well, what do you want? What the heck do you expect of me? Want me to give away my bike? Would that satisfy you? How about the stereo? What do you want?'"

"See that balding older man over there?" I asked. "I wish you would go over and explain that sermon to him in words of one syllable. He didn't get it. But thank God, you got it."

The Last Word: Insights About the Church and Ministry, Abingdon Press, 2000

24

Is Jesus Serious?

Once upon a time, there was a rich man (and you know how we despise the rich) who got word that his manager was pilfering. So, he summoned the little guy for an audit.

"What's this I hear? Show me the books!"

"Er, Boss, uh, nothin' would please me more than to show you the books—I need to do a few...calculations."

The little weasel thinks to himself, *I'm too proud to beg and too weak to do any real work. What am I to do? I've got it! I'll call in my master's debtors and have them write down their debts. They'll be so grateful that, when my master sacks me, I can go to them for help.*

Thus, the swindle begins. Each of the debtors is summoned and asked, "You owe the master $1,000? Let's mark that down to $250. How you like them numbers? Remember this face when you're asked for money for my bail."

Huge sums of money are written off.

Then comes the day of judgment. Now the little wretch will get what his thievery deserves. The dishonest manager presents the cooked books to the master. The master responds with, "You...you *genius*, you! Wow! What wonderful initiative. What commercial creativity. What innovative bookkeeping. I wish all my people were as smart in looking after their future."

Now, what kind of Savior would have told a story like that to people like us? (Though John Wesley said in *Notes on the New Testament*, "I can't believe our Lord would have told a story like this," yep, Jesus really did tell this story.)

Did you hear the one about the man traveling from Jerusalem to Jericho who was mugged, beaten, stripped naked, and left to die like a dog in a ditch?

Now, by chance, down the road comes a priest, a religious official, a man who makes his living off of God—and you know how we all despise clergy. He espies the man bleeding, lying helpless in the ditch, and the priest...passes by on the other side.

Then comes down the road a pious but not priggish, religious but not showy, ordinary Methodist person who, catching a whiff of the now putrefying mess in the ditch, and being religious and therefore quite a cautious sort of person...passes by on the other side.

This is great! Go get 'em Jesus!

Imagine you are the man in the ditch. You've lost a lot of blood. Time is running out. With your last ounce of energy, you look down that hot, dusty road and see coming toward you—a nice-looking, spiritual but not fanatical, probably Republican, traditional-values person like you? No. You see a despised, good-for-nothing, racially impure, theologically uninformed *Samaritan*. Your last best hope is a man whom you hate.

And despite your weak protests—"It's only a flesh wound. I'm okay, I'm okay"—this lousy Samaritan rips up his designer suit, lays your bleeding carcass on the fine leather seats of his Porsche, takes you to the hospital, shells out all of his credit cards, and tells them to spare no expense in your salvation.

"Go and do likewise," says Jesus.

Is this some kind of a joke?

"Only a Savior Like Jesus Could Love People Like You," sermon, Duke University Chapel, September 18, 2011

25

Why There Are No Dogs in Divinity School

In the early days, before seminaries, all the preachers were dogs.

Believe it or not, back then, dogs were quite loquacious. They loved to talk and were really good at it. Their voices carried all over town. So, it was quite natural for them to be drawn toward homiletics as a profession. These canine preachers traveled throughout the land, day and night, preaching. They specialized in leading evening worship.

Some of their sermons were short; some were long. Some of their homilies were delivered in a high-pitched, yelping sort of way that appealed to the emotions of many. The homilies of the big dogs thundered forth. No public address systems were needed.

Most of the dogs preached without notes, maintaining good eye contact, since, though the dogs spoke well, none of them could read. I guess the Lord figured, *Why do they need to read when I've made them that good at speaking?*

In many sermons, dogs treated everyday matters, moral quandaries related to marriages, the need to compost, and taking responsibility for the environment. Other sermons were more theoretical and theological. Subjects like eschatology, doctrines of creation, inspiration, and hamartiology, and angelology were treated and well-illustrated with scenes from daily life.

Then the preachers' sermons took a turn that proved to be their undoing. The preachers began offering advice.

The guidance of the advice-giving, canine preachers was well-received. People got instruction on what they needed to do to have better relationships, stronger family life, purpose-driven lives, job contentment, chaste and obedient kids, satisfying and fulfilling sex, and biblically based business practices—and how to vote in upcoming elections. One Great Dane preached a two-month-long series entitled, "If You Are Depressed, Here's How to Get Happy." It was amazing that, just by being dogs, they were experts on everything.

Eventually, people tired of the constant barrage of moralizing and unwanted counsel. "Just because he's a border collie, he thinks he's a genius," one layperson complained of his preacher after a sermon on "Six Ways to Make Marriage Less Miserable."

"Who's she to be telling us how to live our personal lives?" asked another. "It's a known fact that she had children through half a dozen fathers, many of whom are from other neighborhoods."

"I was okay with my preacher's political opinions, since, like him, I'm a fiscal conservative, then I found out that when he's not preaching, he chases cars. UPS trucks are his Achilles' heel. Then, when he bit our neighborhood letter carrier, I said, 'That's the last straw.'"

As far as we know, that's when the Lord stepped in and ended the preaching life of dogs. Almost overnight, dogs forgot how to talk. Puppies showed no interest in studying homiletics. Content just to wag their tails and bark, none studied preaching as a career. In a short time, there were no sermons being given by dogs, though one collie continued to draw big congregations in Houston for at least a decade.

26

Send a Preacher to Camp

In a world of confusing change, amid the disappearance of time-honored values, it is good to know that some institutions are still pursuing the same noble purposes they did when we were young. The Boy Scouts, for example, are still introducing young people to the joys of nature, the pride of personal achievement, and the breakup of Western civilization, along with the nervous breakdown of the adults who accompany them to camp.

Take me, for instance.

What could I say when Bill Beckman, scoutmaster of Troop 451, called and proposed that I join him as an adult leader for a week at Camp Daniel Boone?

"Besides," said Bill, "everyone else is *working*."

I couldn't protest, knowing that Bill routinely gives up vacations, weekends, and one or two weeks every summer to take my son camping. What can you say about someone who gives that much to work with boys aged eleven to seventeen?

You can say that he has lousy judgment. At least that was what I was thinking when we gathered with eighteen boys in the parking lot to load their gear and head for Canton, the town nearest Daniel Boone. *What have I done?* I wondered as I watched them load sleeping bags, backpacks, knives, hatchets, and machetes into my car. *Are we making an assault on Canton or going there to camp?*

"My son responds best to structured environments," said a mother who was holding tightly her eleven-year-old. "Will the boys be adequately supervised?"

"Dr. Willimon will be going with us," said Bill. "Does that make you feel any better?"

She didn't answer. "Remember, dear, your father and I are only a telephone call away," she said, hugging her son.

"Have you ever done any camping before?" asked the senior patrol leader, looking at me the way he might look at a person who dressed in an evening gown for mud wrestling.

"Sure, I have," I said in an offended tone. "I have done lots of camping and was even an Eagle Scout myself."

"That was a long time ago, though, right?" asked the boy. "A real long time."

It's going to be a long week.

Camp Daniel Boone is located in a beautiful, high-mountain valley. I had been there one weekend, more than thirty years ago, when I was a scout. I expected the place to have changed a lot.

Not a chance. The Boy Scout organization appears to have a fear of plumbing. Give boys plumbing and there's no telling where it will lead next. Camp latrines haven't changed. Nor have the steel, double-decker bunk beds, open-faced shelters, or the gnats and chiggers.

"Isn't this just like *Call of the Wild*?" said Bill as he rolled out his sleeping bag on the bunk.

Sounds more like Lord of the Flies *to me*, I thought as I pondered a week with a group of adolescent males who were preparing to be certified in archery, shotgun and rifle shooting, and hatchet and knife throwing.

"Class A uniform for all evening meals, guys," said Scoutmaster Beckman. "That includes you, Willimon."

"But I don't have a uniform."

"Yes, you do. I brought you one. Remember, you're supposed to be an example to the boys."

He then produced an adult leader's uniform. I emerged from our shelter adorned in scout olive drab—tight shirt, neckerchief, too-short pants, red cap, and knee socks with red tops.

"Knee socks are not meant for somebody your age," remarked the senior patrol leader.

"Thanks for the support," I said.

Dinner that night consisted of chicken and dumplings. The scouts from Florida had never seen anything like it.

"There's great big globs of dough floating around in sauce!" one shouted. "I've stepped in it, but I've never eaten it," said another. Culture shock.

Camp food has not improved since I was a kid. The purpose of the rigorous activities is to make campers so famished that they will eat anything, which they eventually do before the end of the week.

We went to bed that night after someone exploded a can of insect repellent in the fire. A prelude to the week ahead. I fell asleep praying that someone back home would desperately need my services sometime in the next twenty-four hours and thereby deliver me from this Land of Lost Boys.

Monday morning, after a breakfast of something floating in something else, we went rappelling. I think the word comes from the French term for "death by hanging." Something in the adolescent male attracts him to activities that are near-death experiences, to instruments that fire lead, to arrows that pierce the flesh, to high cliffs, to raging rivers. Whenever the boys described a camp activity as "stupid," that meant it had a socially redemptive value, such as fulfilling the merit badges for Nature or Citizenship. Whenever they pronounced an activity "awesome," it meant that there was a high probability that a person could be maimed for life while performing it. The phrase "responsible young person" is an oxymoron.

As with all the other activities, rappelling was led by a college student who was a former scout. He explained the intricacies of rappelling, which consist mainly of strapping yourself around the groin, being coaxed up the face of a rock by someone whom you have just met, while shouting things like "On ballet," (er, "On belay?") and "Up rope."

My apprehension about my first venture into rappelling was not eased by the fact that, on the hike up to the rock, I had had a striking conversation with the rappelling instructor.

"Are you a college student?" I asked him, surveying his 230-plus pounds, which had been poured into a pair of scout shorts, a Daniel Boone T-shirt that exposed his stomach, and topped with a red cap.

"Yessir," he responded.

"Which college?" I asked. "I'm at a college myself."

"It's in Florida," he answered.

"What's its name?" I persisted.

"Well, I can't remember just now. You see, I've just transferred there."

I did not look forward to rappelling with this person.

I am terrified of heights. I am unable to ascend a stepladder, and often feel queasy even up in the pulpit (a malady also suffered by many in my congregation while I am preaching). But I knew not to let the boys know that I was afraid. Show any sign of fear and these people may pounce. So, trying not to look as terrified as I was, I prepared to ascend the face of the rock with the rest of them.

Everyone before me scaled the rock and rappelled down as adroitly as mountain goats, except for the little boy whose mother had challenged me in the parking lot. He looked as terrified as I felt. We were the last to go.

"There is nothing to fear," I said to him, patting him on the back in a fatherly way and amazed at my ability to lie so easily to one so young. "You're in good hands. The guy up at the top knows what he is doing," I said, remembering that the man at the top did not even know where he was attending college.

The poor little boy was able to get up to the top. But on his way back down he lost his toehold and slipped down the face of the rock a few feet, dangling in the air and screaming with fear. We all reassured him that he was fine. He finally got his hold again and made it to the bottom, where I met him. He was trembling with fear and beginning to cry uncontrollably.

"Don't make me do that again. I can't do it again," he pleaded. I comforted him, aware that the other boys were watching him. I called over one of the older boys.

"How about trying to help him?" I said. "See if you can settle him down. He's had a real scare. See if you can reassure him. I don't want him to call his mother. Understand?"

"Yessir," said the older scout. "I'll reassure him."

He put his arm around the shoulder of the younger scout and led him away. I was touched.

Just before they were beyond earshot, I heard the older boy say to the still-whimpering tenderfoot, "Shut up, you little crybaby, or I'll put my fist in your face."

The boy ceased crying immediately and became totally composed.

Now it was my turn to scale the rock. I strapped up and began to struggle upward, all the while remembering that my life was in the hands of a student who couldn't remember the name of his college. Gradually, step by agonizing step, I progressed, not daring to look down. Finally, I could see my counselor, all 230 pounds of him, pulling on the rope attached to my groin, coaxing me to the top. Just then, my foot slipped, and I dangled for a terrifying moment in space, suspended between earth and heaven.

It was then that I heard a reassuring word from the young man at the top, holding the other end of the rope and wearing the red cap: "Hey, move it lard a**, we haven't got all day."

I can't recall how long it has been since I had been referred to in that tone of voice or by that designation. I will probably be a better, more interesting, certainly humbler person because of this.

There is absolutely no limit of good that could come to the practice of homiletics, to ministerial ethics and the mental hygiene of clergy, by sending preachers like me to places like Camp Daniel Boone, there to have their character edified by people who, by all standards of civilized behavior, are mentally unbalanced, wearing olive drab knee socks with red tops.

Send a preacher to camp.

The Christian Century,
November 8, 1989

27

I Was Vanna's Pastor

The other day, I was standing in the supermarket checkout line, madly perusing the latest *Star* magazine in an attempt to finish the article "Vanna Says Nude Photo Is Cheap Shot" before I arrived at the cash register. The woman behind me bumped me with her cart and said, "Either move up in line and pay for it like everybody else, buddy, or let me by."

I turned and said to her in an indignant tone, "Madam, I'll have you know that you are addressing Vanna White's former pastor." She shrieked, and then asked for my autograph. Everything came to a halt in the supermarket as people crowded around me.

Before it was all over, the manager had given me a free copy of the *Star* after I promised always to shop at his store.

Although the *Star* doesn't report it, and you probably will not read about it in her new, long-awaited and hot autobiography, *Vanna Speaks*, it is true: *I was Vanna White's pastor.* The glamorous but taciturn beauty who turns letters on *Wheel of Fortune* was a leader in my church's youth group in North Myrtle Beach, South Carolina.

I admit that I can't exactly detect the influence of my preaching when I watch Vanna turn her letters on *Wheel of Fortune.* About the most they let Vanna say about theology is, "Big money! Big money!" But I am sure that my stamp is there, however subtly.

I expect that her autobiography will contain no mention of my ministerial influence. When David Letterman asked Vanna about the most interesting men she has met, she mentioned only Merv Griffin and Tom Selleck. Perhaps she has forgotten my powerful sermons, or the fascinating course on "Christian Sex, Dating, and Marriage" I gave the youth every year.

Perhaps Vanna never speaks about me because she remembers the advice I gave her. One Sunday in May of her senior year at North Myrtle Beach High, I asked, "Vanna, what are you planning after graduation?" She replied, in her unfailingly sweet and sincere way, that she had always dreamed of going into modeling, so she was going to modeling school in Atlanta.

"Vanna, no!" I said. (I flunked nondirective counseling in seminary.) "Don't do that! Those schools will do nothing but take your money. Nobody ever gets a job after one of those places. You have brains! Ability! You could be more than a model!"

She thanked me politely and said, "But I have this dream of going to Hollywood and becoming an actress."

"From North Myrtle Beach?" I asked. "Vanna, that only happens in movies. This is crazy! I see nursing as a more appropriate career for you."

According to the *Star,* Vanna makes more in two days of taping *Wheel of Fortune* than I make in a whole year of giving good advice to aspiring teenagers.

The Christian Ministry, January 1987

28
Just Say No

Some pastors find it utterly impossible to say no. The word is not in their clerical vocabulary, the sad result of Tillichian acceptance of their acceptance, accepting everything gone wild, I suppose. Oh, they mean and want to say no, but someone—a parishioner, a bishop, the president of the PTA—will say, "Oh, please don't refuse us. It won't take much of your time. Besides, everyone else is *working*."

Then begins the pitiful process of self-doubt, insecurity, and the general ministerial desire to please, leading to the inevitable. "Well, I suppose I could, just this once. What harm would it do? It might even do some good, and I so want to do good."

I think the pastor with the worst case of this was the Reverend Adrian Smollett, who served my Aunt Agnes's church. He shouldn't have gone there; he knew he would be miserable, but the bishop called and Smollett couldn't refuse. From the day he arrived, the congregation quickly realized that Smollett was an easy mark. At his past church, Smollett's damning agreeableness had brought him, and the congregation, to grief. He had resolved not to let it happen here. But scarcely had he unpacked his belongings when the trouble began.

"I want you to visit with me at Rotary," said the chairperson of the administrative board. Smollett had his fill of civic clubs, with their brooms, pancakes, and booths at football games, at his previous post and therefore replied, "Thank you. It's nice of you to ask, and I do want to be active in the community. But I like to keep my lunch hour open."

"Come now, man," said his tormentor. "Surely you can't be busy every day at noon." Smollett was too polite to lie and too full of grace to say no. He capitulated. He was now not only a Methodist but also a Rotarian.

But then what was he to say to other church members who invited him to Civitan, Lions, Ruritan, and the Full Gospel Business Men's Fellowship? Smollett said yes to them all. As a result, he took only two meals a week with his family. He was always brimming with English peas, sliced turkey, and misery.

But eventually Smollett's fatal flaw caught up with him. The church officers didn't balk when he took over every job in the church. ("Quite a go-getter we have for a preacher," they would brag in town.) But they began to take a more critical look at Smollett's ministry among them. Many opposed the color he painted the church fellowship hall. They were cruel to blame Smollett. Someone had mentioned how much money they could save if "someone who really loves the Lord" painted the room. Smollett took the bait, grabbed a brush, and got busy. Sadly, Smollett used paint that was on sale at the hardware store; the hall was painted half OSHA-approved orange and the other half light peach.

Through it all, Smollett managed to perform six weddings a week, welcoming all comers, and ten funerals for an assortment of Buddhists, Muslims, and those who follow the spiritual teachings of Shirley MacLaine.

His end came, not as everyone had predicted, from overwork and fatigue, but from an infected cat bite that he received at the St. Francis Day Blessing of the Animals Service. On the day he died, he passed in and out of consciousness, alert just long enough to marry a couple who were passing through town on their way to Atlanta. He also managed to address the weekly luncheon of nursing students by way of the hospital's closed-circuit TV system.

Toward the end, he raved incoherently, "Yes, that is, I suppose...perhaps I could...No, I'm not all that busy...Yes, more peas, please, and perhaps just a tiny slice of your wonderful cake...It is a joy to be able to address you tonight...No, I don't really mind..."

Then Smollett breathed his last.

His soul was seen trudging toward the place of eternal bliss, resigned, yet confident that he would be granted divine affirmation.

The Christian Ministry,
September–October 1989

Suggested by Stephen Leacock's
The Awful Fate of Melpomenus Jones

29

Quitting Time?

It was the last Sunday of the school year, and the phone was ringing at eight o'clock in the morning. "Hello," I answered.

"Dr. Willimon, are you awake yet?" the undergraduate chapel attendant asked.

"Yes, of course I'm awake," I responded, taking offense.

"Just wanted you to know there's no electricity in the chapel."

"What? No electricity? Is it dark?"

"Well, I had to get a flashlight in order to dial your number."

"That dark? Has the choir arrived yet?"

"I can hear people moving around down front, but I can't see anybody."

I rushed across town and arrived at a still totally dark chapel. "Quick! Go downstairs and get your hands on every candle we have—the used ones in the storage room, in the closet, and everywhere," I told those milling about.

After a hectic forty-five minutes of scurrying around, we had about three hundred fifty candles lit, occupying every flat surface in the chapel.

The candles only barely broke the darkness of the huge Gothic-style building. Having no electricity for the organ, we completely changed the service to accommodate a piano we muscled in from a nearby building. Fifteen minutes before the service was to begin, I was wringing wet with perspiration from shifting furniture and rewriting the service.

Then, in answer to someone's prayer—not mine at this point—the electricity and all the lights snapped on. This meant that as the majority of worshippers arrived, they were greeted by a fully illuminated chapel filled with three hundred fifty burning candles.

"Well, well. Candles?" said some smart-aleck sophomore as he entered the chapel. "What has dramatic Dr. Willimon in store for us today, Radio City Music Hall? The Rockettes?"

"Sit down and shut up" was my pastoral response.

Matters got worse. In all the confusion beforehand, I had forgotten to put on my robe for the processional. The musicians were confused, singing some hymns I thought we'd dropped, dropping other hymns I thought we'd retained. Cues were missed. The whole thing was a mess. I couldn't wait for the service to limp to its sorry conclusion.

Toward the end of the service, as I sat in my seat, I thought, *There has got to be an easier way of making a living. This is ridiculous. God has no interest in a church at this location. I have to find some less stressful line of work.*

Finally, I said the benediction, and the congregation filed out of the chapel.

"I loved the candles," said one freshman. "Nice touch."

After everyone had gone, three undergraduate women approached me. "Dr. Willimon, we are all seniors," one of them said. "We are graduating next week. As we've thought about our time here at the university, we consider Sundays in the chapel as among our best memories. We are going to miss these Sundays. We wanted to thank you for enriching our lives and helping us during our years here."

Here I was, all prepared to throw in the towel and admit defeat, having convinced myself that Christian ministry is completely futile, pointless, and utterly ineffective. So, God sends these three wonderful people to tell me their lives have been touched through this ministry.

I don't know whether to be disgusted or grateful.

The Christian Ministry,
July–August 1990

30
A Child's Sermon

It was a cold Christmas Eve a few years ago, and my family was running late for the communion service. Where are my sermon notes? Who has my collar? Don't forget to turn off the lights; do you think I'm made of money? Everybody in the car and keep quiet.

On the way to church, my five-year-old daughter, who had been looking rather pale all day, finally got sick, throwing up in the car. *Great*, I thought. *If people only knew what preachers go through.*

I wheeled into the church parking lot and jumped out, leaving my wife, Patsy, to clean up the car and get the kids into church. If people only knew what preachers' spouses go through.

Patsy led a still unsteady and pale Harriet into the church, suggesting that they sit on the back pew, in the darkness, in case she got sick again. Our son William, age seven, ran down to the front of the church to join his visiting grandparents.

I hastily threw on my robe, took a deep breath, and joined the choir for the processional. I made it through the first part of the service, and the sermon. Then came the Eucharist. I prayed, broke the bread, poured the wine, and invited everyone forward for communion.

Patsy said it never occurred to her to suggest that Harriet go forward to receive communion. After all, she wasn't feeling well, despite it being the night before Christmas. Patsy went down, then returned to her seat in the darkened rear of the church. She noticed William get up from where he was sitting and go back to the communion rail. What was he up to? She watched him race to the back of the church and scoot down the pew toward his sister.

He opened his hands, revealing a small piece of bread. "Harriet, the body of Christ, given for you."

Without hesitating, she picked the bread out of his hands and plopped it into her mouth, saying, "Amen."

William slid back down the pew and ran to join his grandparents.

I don't mean to be sentimental, and I hate it when we preachers tell cute stories about our kids, but I must ponder that, when God Almighty chose to come among us, God chose to come as a child.

As a big, grown-up, responsible adult, I am quite adept at making myself the center of the world, turning even religion into something that revolves around me and my big, adult responsibilities. I get consumed by the necessary, the required, the expected, and the accustomed; sometimes I forget to pay attention. So, God sends a child as a harbinger ("this shall be a sign unto you"), like a road sign pointing the way, or a stop sign to halt us dead in our tracks, someone to get our attention.

One day Jesus was walking with his disciples, teaching them. All were taking notes, trying hard to pay attention. They said to Jesus, "Can't something be done about these children? Send them to children's church or the nursery or something. They are distracting."

Remember what Jesus did? He put a child in the middle of them and said, "When you receive one such child [surprise!] you receive me."

The child is here to distract us from our big, serious, but utterly self-centered adult religion, in order that baby Jesus might get our attention and lead us toward a kingdom that, according to him, has a very small door through which only the small can enter.

The Christian Ministry,
January–February 1990

31

Children's Sermon

I was visiting a congregation where, during the Sunday service, the preacher indulged in a practice not dear to my heart—a "children's sermon." The boys and girls were called down front.

Squatting in the chancel, the preacher began: "Boys and girls, today is Epiphany. Can you say *Epiphany*? Epiphany falls on January 6, but today it falls on Sunday. Isn't that great, boys and girls? Epiphany means 'revelation,' 'manifestation.' A favorite Epiphany story is found at the beginning of Matthew's Gospel. You know the story. It's the story of the wise men who came to Bethlehem to see the baby Jesus. But they weren't really 'wise men' or even 'three kings.' The Bible calls them magi. Magi. That's where we get our word *magic*. They were magicians, astrologers (the kind Mrs. Reagan uses). [No laughter in congregation.] They came 'from the East.' Some people think they came from Persia. Boys and girls, where is Persia? [Silence. One child ventures, "Iran?"]

"Yes. Iran. Good. That was Persia, but it wasn't all of Persia. What other countries are located in what was Persia?" One child says, "Iraq?"

"Iraq! Good! Iraq. In fact, some people think these magi came from Baghdad, capital of Iraq. There were lots of these magi in Iraq.

"And Matthew says these magi, these Iraqis, *were the first to get an Epiphany, the first to see and to worship the baby Jesus.* A lot of people who had the Bible, a lot of people who thought they were close to God, missed it, and these strange people from Iraq saw it."

After a "little prayer," when the boys and girls were sent back to their parents in the pews, I noted that the congregation was fumbling for seatbelts. You tell a story like that, Sunday, 11:15 a.m., you don't know where we'll be headed by noon.

That sweet little children's sermon was preached on January 6, 1991, as the bombs were beginning to fall on Baghdad.

The Last Word: Insights About the
Church and Ministry, Abingdon Press, 2000

32
Church Growth

We decided that we needed to grow. We voted to launch a program of evangelism. Evangelism, you know what that means. It's the "We-had-better-go-out-and-get-new-members-or-we'll-die" syndrome. Beginning in the 1960s, our church had begun a two-decade decline in membership, so we figured that a little church-growth strategy was in order.

We studied a program from our denomination telling us how to get new members. Among other things, the church-growth program advocated a system of door-to-door visitation. So, we organized ourselves into groups of two and, on an appointed Sunday afternoon, we set out to visit, to invite people to our church.

The teams went out, armed with packets of pamphlets describing our congregation, pamphlets telling about our denomination, fliers portraying me, the smiling pastor, inviting people to our church. Each team was given a map with the team's assigned street.

Helen and Gladys were given a map. They were clearly told to go down Summit Drive and to *turn right*. That's what they were told. I heard the team leader tell them, "You go down Summit Drive and turn right. Do you hear me, Helen? That's down Summit Drive and turn right?"

But Helen and Gladys, both approaching eighty, after lifetimes of teaching elementary school, were better at giving than receiving directions. They turned left, venturing down into the housing projects to the west of Summit Drive.

Which meant that Helen and Gladys proceeded to evangelize the wrong neighborhood and thereby ran the risk of evangelizing the wrong people.

Late that afternoon, each team returned to the church to make its report. Helen and Gladys had only one interested person to report to us, a woman named Verleen. Nobody on their spurious route was interested in visiting our church, nobody but Verleen. She lived with her two children in a three-room apartment in the projects, we were told. Although she had never been to a church in her life, Verleen wanted to visit ours.

This is what you get, I said to myself, when you don't follow directions, when you won't do what the pastor tells you to do; this is what you get, a woman from the projects named Verleen.

Next Sunday, Helen and Gladys proudly presented Verleen at the eleven o'clock service, Verleen along with two feral-looking children. Verleen liked the service so much, she said, that she wanted to attend the women's Thursday-morning Bible study. Helen and Gladys said they would pick her up.

On Thursday, Verleen appeared, proudly clutching her new Bible, a gift of Helen's circle, the first Bible Verleen had ever seen, much less owned.

I was leading the study that morning, a study on the lection for the coming Sunday: Luke 4, the story of Jesus's temptation in the wilderness. "Have any of you ever been faced with temptation and, with Jesus's help, resisted?" I asked the group after presenting my material. "Have any of you refused some temptation because of your Christian commitment?"

One of the women told about how, just the week before, there was some confusion in the supermarket checkout line and, before she knew it, she was standing in the supermarket parking lot with a loaf of bread that she had not paid for.

"At first I thought," she confessed, "Why should I pay for it? They have enough money as it is. But then I thought, 'No, you are a Christian.' So I went back in the store and paid them for that loaf of bread."

I murmured some approving comment.

It was then that Verleen spoke. "A couple of years ago I was into cocaine really big. You know what that's like! You know how that stuff makes you crazy. Well, anyway, my boyfriend—not the one I've got now, the one who was the daddy of my first child, that one—well, we knocked over a gas station one night—got $200 out of it. It was as simple as taking candy from a baby. Well, my boyfriend, he says to me, 'Let's knock off that 7-Eleven down on the corner.' And something in me says, 'No, I've held up that gas station with you, but I ain't going to hold up no convenience store.' He beat the hell out of me, but I still said no. It felt great to say no, 'cause that's the only time in my life I ever said no to anything. Made me feel like I was somebody."

Through the stunned silence I managed to mutter, "Well, er, uh, that's resisting temptation. That's sort of what this text is about. And now it's time for our closing prayer."

After I stumbled out of the church parlor and was standing out in the parking lot helping Helen into her car, she said to me, "Can't wait to get home and get on the phone and invite people to come next Thursday! Your Bible studies used to be dull. I think I can get a good crowd for this!"

I didn't know whether to laugh or cry. But the church, by the grace of God, grew.

The Intrusive Word, William B. Eerdmans Publishing Company, 1994

33

The Church Argumentative

It's summer. Time for iced tea, softball, walks on the beach, trips to the mountains. Down here in South Carolina, it's time also for mosquitoes, poison ivy, chiggers, heat stroke, and annual statewide church meetings.

Being Christian is tough enough here as it is; a herculean effort when I'm cornered with a thousand other United Methodists in our annual conference at Spartanburg, sharing dormitory showers at Wofford College.

Each year in early June we enact the truth of the old dictum that says, "Methodist preachers are like manure: spread them around and they do a lot of good; pile them together in one place and they get to stinking."

United Methodists are organized (using "organize" very loosely) into annual conferences presided over by bishops. Each summer we get together, sing, shout, hear interminable reports, and maneuver for our next pastoral appointment. The lively debates are often more heat than light. "Bishop, tell me again what was the question?" one delegate asked after he had monopolized the microphone for a full five minutes of harangue.

We've got a rule that positive and negative speeches on a given motion must alternate. More than once, after some impassioned utterance, Bishop Roy Clark had to ask, "Was that supposed to be for or against the motion?"

After one meandering tirade by a fellow minister, I overheard one lay delegate whisper to another, "If you think that speech was hard to follow, you ought to hear his sermons."

In the course of one hot afternoon, we argued the merits of the Equal Rights Amendment, military intervention in El Salvador, capital punishment, and the morality of paying $10,000 to get "How Great Thou Art" in *The Methodist Hymnal*. We still had time to consider the abolition of prepackaged condiments in Methodist nursing homes ("That's '*condiments*,' Bishop—ketchup, mustard, things of that nature. Not what you're thinking. I tell you, if you could see these dear, arthritic hands attempting to open a package of mustard..."). A resolution ("Be it resolved that no United Methodist shall tamper with the original tongue of the Holy Scriptures") went down in defeat.

When a member of our conference Board of Church and Society predicted that "the world will note what we say here today," I went out in the lobby to a pay phone and called a Presbyterian buddy of mine to confirm that. He didn't even know we were meeting.

The debate on the floor was nothing compared to the debates out in the lobby. That's where real business takes place—when we can hug somebody into our point of view.

Through it all, Bishop Clark maintained civility and patience that made us wonder about his contact with reality.

Through all the backslapping and arguing and brouhaha, there were moments of gracious divine intrusion. At the recognition service for those retiring from the ministry, one man said, "Got paid $200 my first year in the ministry; next year they cut it in half."

In all the singing, praying, shouting, and three-point speeches, this, believe it or not, is my beloved church doing its business. At a time of growing division, it's great to see folks argue with and preach to one another solely on the basis that they are all trying to follow Jesus.

Acts 15 says we've been doing this sort of thing for a long time. At that primal Jerusalem Conference, before Paul and Barnabas arrived, there was "no small dissension" among the delegates. After Paul and Barnabas got to the microphone, there was even more ferocious wrangling (Rom 9–11). At last, through some skillful maneuvers by Paul and (so Luke says) some compromises suggested by, of all people, Peter, the dust settled. It "seemed good to the Holy Spirit and to us" to seek the open way on the Gentile issue. Those on the losing side swallowed their pride, all stood and sang one verse of "Blest Be the Tie That Binds," hugged, turned in their dormitory room keys, and the church moved on.

Bishop Clark, take heart. It don't get closer to a Spirit-led church than that.

The Christian Century,
July 29–August 5, 1981

34

The Dog Days of Pentecost

It's hot around here right now—dead hot. The summer, which began so pleasantly with picnics and trips to the beach in June, has bogged down in hot, muggy August heat. No one wants to go anywhere; even the beach is unappealing. Few venture beyond sight of an air conditioner or a glass of iced tea. We're in the late-summer doldrums, the dog days of summer.

Around the church, life is even slower and less eventful. Attendance is down, along with giving. The choir will not meet again until September. Sunday services are lethargic and dull. "God hasn't taken a vacation," declares the bulletin board outside my neighbor's church—but the people certainly have. And I'm not all that sure about God, either. To judge from the way things look around here, God may have thrown in the towel along with everybody else and moved to cooler climes until fall. I wouldn't blame him. Those of us who have already taken our vacations are left here to mind the church until everybody else gets back.

As I planned for next Sunday's sermon, the epistle lesson had a peculiar relevance. The epistle for the twelfth Sunday after Pentecost is Hebrews 12:1-6. Consider the context of that letter. The Hebrews had been plodding along, year after year, waiting for that promised Second Coming. But what had changed? Caesar still ruled; the faithful still suffered and died. Their unbelieving neighbors either ignored them or taunted them, saying, "Where is your Lord? Why doesn't your God get busy and do something?"

For the Hebrews, it was a time of uneventful waiting, a weary cooling of the church's heels in the doldrums of unfulfilled expectations. They had not paid for their faith in blood; no dramatic, barbaric persecutions had tested them. But they were paying a price. I think my church and I know something of that cost of discipleship.

Chapter 11 contains that memorable roll call of the heroes of the faith. "Faith" is best defined by the lives of the faithful. "So then," begins chapter 12, "let's also run the race that is laid out in front of us, since we have such a great cloud of witnesses surrounding us" (Heb 12:1). Jesus is the "pioneer" who has gone before us in his suffering, enabling us suffering ones to run with confidence (12:2-3).

But the difficulty with all this talk about running is that the Hebrews aren't getting anywhere. Unlike some of the other saints, they have not been "disciplined" by martyrdom and violent persecution (12:4). Nevertheless, they have been tested simply by their long, uneventful, undramatic wait. Their "race" has been mostly a hot, bleak trek through the Slough of Despond rather than a martyr's dash to glory. And they have found that the way is long.

Where I live, in these dog days of summer, as August plods wearily to a close and our church life drags along uneventfully, I think I am learning with those Hebrews what it means to wait. Pentecost season begins so dramatically, with raucous shouts, visions, tongues of fire. The church is born and reborn amid the giddy-headed drunkenness of the Spirit's descent and optimistic talk about joy, power, and all things being held in common. But the fire of Pentecost soon becomes the swelter-ing heat of the summer sun. The old song "Beneath the Cross of Jesus" speaks of the "burning of the noontide heat and the burden of the day." Such unfulfillment is a cross to bear.

To be martyred by fire before screaming pagans is one way to pay for the faith, but I submit that it's also tough to pay, day by day, in a lonely, dull, ignored-by-pagans wilting that comes from waiting. Our denominations lose both members and triumphalist visions. Billy Gra-ham's continually promised revival of religion does not come, and my pagan neighbors react to us Christians with indifference or a polite, secularist yawn. For our church, it is neither the hopeful first light of dawn nor the brilliant, apocalyptic hues of sunset—it is the relentless mugginess of late afternoon. And who wants to go anywhere in weather like this?

The "race," if our loping along can be called a race, is hard. It's hard because, unlike some of the heroes before us, we're not racing against bloody executioners: *we are racing against our own despair, weariness, and disappointment.* We are fighting the nagging, chronic, ordinary lack of fulfillment of our hope. Such wait requires discipline, the discipline of faith which trusts, endures, continues to name the Name and tell the Story even when the hope is unfulfilled and the world keeps reminding us that it's not listening anyway. Discipline is required—a commodity that is in as short supply in the church as anywhere else today.

Old Screwtape knew. In writing to his young devil, the satanic mentor declared that, in the fight against Christians, time itself is the best ally:

> It is so hard for these creatures to persevere. The routine of adversity, the gradual decay of youthful loves and youthful hopes, the quiet despair (hardly felt as pain) of ever overcoming the chronic temptations with which we have again and again defeated them, the drabness which we create in their lives, and the inarticulate resentment with which we teach them to respond to it—all this provides admirable opportunities for wearing out a soul by attrition. (*The Screwtape Letters*, C. S. Lewis)

Hebrews has it right: "perseverance" (12:1 NRSV) is what's needed in the dog days of the church—stubborn, hard-headed determination, after all, may be what the letter to the Hebrews suggests that faith itself really is. For how does one live by something so intangible as "the assurance of things hoped for, the conviction of things not seen" (11:1 NRSV) except by sheer stubbornness? *Tentatio* was the elegant Latin word by which the Scholastics spoke of this tenacious brand of trust. Nobody will see God, they declared, except the hardheaded, the stubborn, and tenacious.

The heroes of faith, at least among the gallery that appears in chapter 11 of Hebrews, are not so much the martyrs as the perseverers— the Abrahams and the Moseses who plodded through a wilderness of drab, uneventful, everyday life; with the noonday sun beating down on their backs, but with eyes fixed on God's postponed future. It was not so much a race they ran as a tedious trek. This "cloud of witnesses" who trudged ahead of us, whose witness was in their perseverance, now sit in the bleachers, cheering us who come after them. "So strengthen your drooping hands and weak knees. Make straight paths for your feet" (12:12-13a).

At the point of my greatest weariness, I think I hear an encouraging shout arising from those seated saints. So, I pour myself another glass of iced tea, go back over next Sunday's sermon one more time, and keep on keeping on. For faithfulness on a hot Pentecost afternoon, this must suffice.

The Christian Century,
August 13–20, 1980

35

God Is a Young Adult, Growing Younger

In the past, God spoke through the prophets to our ancestors in many times and many ways. In these final days, though, he spoke to us through a Son.

Hebrews 1:1-2

No one has ever seen God, say the scriptures. We still want to.

So, God gave us preachers to testify that God, the Hidden One, refuses to stay obscure, arcane, and ineffable. Scripture dares metaphor—God the Rock, Mighty Warrior, Mother Hen, the pursuing, overwrought Lover in evening in a fragrant garden, mighty wind who makes oaks to whirl, Good Shepherd, King of Kings, Bloody Lamb, Woman tearing her house apart searching for one lost coin.

Everyone knows not to take such poetry literally. Still…what if Freud, Marx, and Marcus Borg are wrong? What if these names, these metaphors, are not solely constructed by us, not our feeble human wish projection? What if (as Karl Barth said) some of these metaphors, maybe all of them for all I know, are given by God, gifts of God's relentless self-disclosure, tireless self-revelation?

In all sorts of ways God spoke to us, but now God has spoken to us as a young adult (see Heb 1:1-2).

God is a young adult just getting started, perpetually in his early thirties, launched, but not quite, forever young. I expect that's a jarring, unwelcomed thought for many, particularly if you are a young woman who has had difficulty with immature men. Even uncomfortable for me: an aging male who feels a threat when around young adult males, a sense of menace.

If you think you have come up with a comfortable, agreeable metaphor for God that works for you—think again. We are inveterate idolaters.

I've searched the scriptures: Jesus says nothing to people my age. True, Luke begins with a couple of old people hanging out at church, Elizabeth, Zechariah, but then sends them back to the home after their bit parts in the beginning of the story of Jesus, never to be heard from again. These Lukan seniors do what people my age ought to do for people under thirty—get out of the way!

God, the One who hung the heavens and flung the planets in their courses, is an adult, but just barely, innocent, bright-eyed, alert, nervous, edgy, and at the peak of his powers. He could do with a shave and a shower.

On Pentecost, the church's birthday, someone had too much to drink, according to the scoffing mob out in the street. Some of the furniture got tossed about in the upper room, there was the scent of smoke (burning hemp?), and everybody began to shout, shake, rattle, and roll—all against house regulations. That's what you sometimes get, I found as a college chaplain, when the kids party.

God is a young adult who may be ADD in his inability to sit still. Watch his legs constantly bouncing nervously, when everyone else in the room is satisfied to be static. In his bounding and rocking, he has the demeanor of a twelve-year-old, not a person at thirty.

Eager, attentive, marveling as if everything is new and awesome, as if all the facts and figures of science, the ancient plays of Shakespeare, a tree full of figs, a seed germinating and taking root, and the poetry of Isaiah were fresh and for his joy alone. One of his best stories is about two boys his age who were both, though in different ways, the father's pain in the neck. Why am I unsurprised that so many of his stories end with parties, one a bash with individuals who are lame, maimed, and blind—people with whom we wouldn't be caught dead on a Saturday night?

He walks too fast, this postadolescent. He invites us to join in. Heck, he invites everybody to walk with him, to join him on an adventure, a road trip to God knows where. We have trouble keeping up with his breathless pace. Along the way, he notices things we have, in our maturity and experience, stopped noticing: a poor beggar, a widow's coin, a wild lily, a disordered child. He calls our attention, as people his age are wont to do, to the mistakes of pompous, self-important adults, is saddened by the injustices of people in power. He calls the president a "fox." He says in public that no one goes in the kingdom of God but kids, and that rich people are virtually impossible to be saved. But with God, well, anything's possible.

With age and increasing experience, we thought, he will be just like us. He'll learn. Change his tune. Mature. Settle down.

We thought wrong.

Like all those who are beginning, he is obsessed with the future. With him, it's all tomorrow. Tradition plays not as large a role in his worldview as we would have liked.

God is a young adult for whom friends are everything. He invites, embraces even those whom he hardly knows. He loves to hang out with his buddies and tends to make most everyone his buddy, particularly those who are buddy to none. Loves to roam, careening from one party to the next where there is too much drinking and the wine runs out and miraculously overflows, and then to move on to the next place where he is uninvited.

Sometimes, at parties, random people come up to him, argue, insult him to his face. Not once does he ever turn anyone away or smack their face, as you would have.

God is a young adult who spends more time with a crowd, a gang, out and about, than alone.

God is a young adult who wants to know us better, has opinions for how we should live our lives. He wants to know us better than we want to know him. Unlike lots of other young adults, he puts himself out there, gives an invitation to the big party, risks rejection. And most whom he invites reject him. Our refusal to let down our guard, get loose, and join the party must make him feel lousy, though he doesn't show it.

Even though we said *no* to him in as nice a way as we know how, and even though we gave him little encouragement, we bet he will call in the morning. Then again, and again, and again; might as well relent and say *yes*.

God is a young adult—inexperienced, outspoken, rash, always in motion, having difficulty settling in, staying on the subject.

He is nothing we expected in God.

Like many his age, he has yet to develop good self-defense mechanisms. He will probably be hurt. Whatever he thinks, he says. Idealistic, innocent, wise beyond his years, always reaching out, ceaselessly seeking contact, wanting to touch, to risk relationship. Loves to stay out late, engage in risky behavior, launch out in the middle of the night, middle of a storm, up all night.

God is a young adult in motion, all potential. Maybe that's the reason he is tough to pin down, define, to fix. He is the polite kid next door who wants to be helpful. He is the guy on the make at the bar your mother warned you about. He is the belligerent, pushy troublemaker itching for an argument. Everybody enjoys hanging out with him; nobody wants to follow him.

God is a young adult: intense, passionate, unbalanced, immoderate, passionate but not as we usually use that word, oddly disinterested in sex, despite what you have heard from the United Methodist General Conference. He may be a thirtysomething, single male, but he doesn't act like most of them when it comes to sex, marriage, and family.

You suspect that he will ingratiate himself to you, tempt you to do things you were warned you never to do, ask you for money. It makes you nervous to be alone with him. Without any encouragement, he will call you, maybe not tomorrow or the next day, but he will call.

God is a young adult who constantly pushes the envelope, tests the bounds of propriety. He is the redneck good old boy calling out, "Hey! Watch this!" before he jumps. He is the unshaven, dark, long-haired, Near Eastern-looking twentysomething behind you in line at the airport. How can a man be that threatening when he is unarmed?

Why couldn't God have matured, settled down, married, become middle-aged, middle-class, *via media*, middle-of-the-road, before God got close and personal? Why didn't God come to us building on the past, moderately? Why this lurch to the left, then to the right, careening into the future, all promise, potential, and forward movement? Disrespectful of tradition and propriety, ever onward, vital, youthful energy confined in a Jew. Why so few opportunities for quiet reflection, meditation, and rest? I didn't know I was aging, hoary, easily fatigued, winded, quickly tired until him. When will he settle down, get a minivan, vote Republican, develop spiritual disciplines, and act like the God we wanted?

God is a young adult whom we did not expect. This much motion, passion, relentlessness of contact, intrusive, boundless intimacy, and energy.

He makes friends quickly and keeps them for eternity. Like many of his generation, he is slow to judge. Did I mention that he has trouble staying in one place long?

God is a young adult who will ask some outrageous favor, even before he knows you that well. Violator of boundaries, he touches, caresses, fondles feet, kisses other men on the mouth, even those who betray him.

He was not in the military, though his "peace" is no peace as people my age define peace. While he never once raised his hand against anybody, something about him made us want him dead.

Journal for Preachers, Advent 2013

36

If You Drink My Water, Love My Town

It's that time of year again. We in the Durham–Chapel Hill area are in the midst of our annual "unexpected" drought. An absence of rain has become as predictable among us as the earnest appeals from our neighbors over in Chapel Hill for water in their time of water deprivation.

"Hey, pal, can you spare five hundred thousand gallons, just to tide us over until September?"

While I'm pleased that we in Durham have enough water to spare, and it's good to do a good deed to once again help Chapel Hill through another dry spell, I've got some nagging doubts in the back of my mind about the wisdom of our annual show of beneficence toward Chapel Hill. Should the citizens of Bull City keep our weaker neighbors afloat through yet another summer? I ask because I'm sick and tired of having my beloved city put down by high-and-mighty neighbors who would be high and dry except for our liquid neighborliness.

We moved to Durham a little over a year ago. Before we had even taken up residence, it became apparent that we were entering a city in the grip of a vast inferiority complex. I've had professional training in pastoral counseling, so I know a complex when I see one.

"Durham is okay," one of my colleagues on the Duke faculty begrudgingly admitted, "but you would like living in Chapel Hill so much better. It's much more civilized. Quaint, even."

When we were wined and dined by the search committee, where did they take us for dinner?

"Durham? Are you kidding? There's nowhere decent to eat in Durham," they scoffed.

So they drove us bumper-to-bumper down a dangerous stretch of four-lane suicide to Chapel Hill, where we endured the condescension of a waiter who bragged that we were lucky to be eating at "the only good restaurant in the area," paying a large price for small portions of wilted broccoli and "beef stroganoff," which looked vaguely like something I remember seeing in the mess line in the army.

This meal was followed by a stroll along Chapel Hill's shops, where we soaked in culture and sophistication, were hooted at by three undergraduates in a light blue jeep, festooned with subversive bumper stickers, and then trudged back to dear old drab Durham. I for one was not impressed by the self-effacing attitude of Durham residents in the presence of the self-conscious, belligerent snobbishness of their suburb to the south.

This novice Durham citizen has had all the condescending, ungrateful-for-Durham's-generosity, hypocritical slurs from Chapel Hill that I can endure. No more fawning over quaintness, no more covetous longing for Chapel Hill chic to replace Durham drab. Citizens of Durham unite! We have nothing to lose but our inferiority complex!

What is this chic culture and sophistication with which Chapel Hill seeks to intimidate and oppress us? It is mostly the pseudosophistication of an effete intelligentsia who have cloistered themselves in a gated community posing as a town. Chapel Hill chic is wearing shoes that make the human foot look like that of a duck and hurt like the devil—unless you sit in a professor's office all day. Chapel Hill chic is driving an old gray Volvo, held together with left-wing bumper stickers, while munching a yogurt wheat germ muffin. Chapel Hill chic is the delight of eating your own vegetables from your own organic garden (grown in packaged manure from the Winn-Dixie store), the joy of living where everyone is liberated, open-minded, deeply concerned, that is, where everyone is just like you.

Chapel Hill chic is the courage of marching in a protest demonstration in bold support of a cause everyone else in Chapel Hill is in favor of. Chapel Hill chic is voting against any city expansion or modernization and then being forced to drive over to Durham to buy a toothbrush in your aging Volvo. It's building bike lanes rather than an adequate town reservoir.

In place of this faux "chic" give me Durham drab any day. Here we have a no-nonsense, gritty utilitarian, no-frills town without pretense or presumption. We are what we are. We would rather eat fried chicken with the Colonel than French cuisine in Chapel Hill.

Durham's problems match those of some of the world's greatest cities. Our crime rate is as high as any major metropolitan area in the country. Here in Durham, intelligence is measured by your ability to get from one end of town to another without once going the wrong way down our one-way streets that all go in the wrong direction.

Every time I step out from my house and catch the aroma of freshly cured tobacco gently hovering over Bull City, or pull my Dodge Dart over to the side of the street to let two police cars trailing three fire trucks trailing one ambulance race past, or spend half a day hunting a book in our downtown dilapidated library (who says Durham doesn't honor the past?), I know I live in a great city.

Last August, during the last water crisis, the very friends who had made such derogatory remarks about my town, who flaunted their "I'd Rather Be In Chapel Hill" bumper stickers, were the very same people who drank nine glasses of water at our dinner party at our home and ended the evening by asking to take a bath in our tub because such acts were now felonies in Chapel Hill.

This year, I'm putting my foot down. You don't drink my water if you don't love my town. Let's see how romantic Chapel Hill appears when it's a $500 fine to flush a toilet.

These days, though the heavens over Chapel Hill may be Carolina blue, the town reservoir is not. Durham drab is looking good. Let's drink to that!

The Durham Morning Herald,
July 24, 1977

37

Admiration for Stupidity

A congregant emerged after service at the church where I was visiting preacher. "I didn't like some of your criticisms of the president. Even though I don't agree with our president on everything, and even though I don't like some of the crude ways he expresses himself, I do admire him for so boldly saying what he thinks," she said to me.

"Where have you been all my life?" I asked. "I've spent my whole ministry hoping to have someone in my congregation like you. I've longed for someone who said of me, 'I don't agree with all the stupid, inappropriate, crude things he says, but how I admire him for saying what he thinks!'

"You wouldn't believe how many dumb things I'm thinking. Thanks for your permission to say them."

38

The Reverend Grandma

Carlyle Marney once said to me, "God will use any handle to get hold of somebody." Divine persistence and resourcefulness are, according to Scripture, virtually without limits. Bessie Parker was the handle God used to take hold of South Carolina for more than three decades until her death two years ago. Bessie, who became a pastor in 1956— first woman to do so—wore out automobiles the way her Methodist circuit-riding ancestors went through horses, routinely driving thirty thousand miles every year. Although she had a reputation for being one of the most effective preachers in the South Carolina Conference of the United Methodist Church, she was the bane of the bishops. Churches complained when they heard that they were getting a "lady preacher"— and they resisted even more obstinately four years later when the bishop dared to move "our dear Preacher Parker" somewhere else.

With snow-white hair and a soothing, Southern drawl, she epitomized everyone's stereotype of a grandmother. This she used for everything it was worth. Preachers stood in line to enlist Bessie to lead their annual mission fund appeals. When she got to preaching, telling congregants how much they were going to enjoy sending breeder pigs down to Haiti ("They will go down there and make more piggies in the name of the Lord," Bessie would giggle), pigs started packing. When one church repeatedly refused to fix its leaking church roof, the members were scandalized one Monday morning by the sight of their pastor, white hair, blue jeans, and all, atop the roof, hammering away. The roof was quickly repaired with everyone's willing assistance. "It just don't look right to have your grandmother up fixing your roof," one church officer commented.

Toward the end of her ministry, the bishop sent Bessie to a very difficult church, one infamous for feuding, contentiousness, racism, and animosity toward the denomination. Before Bessie arrived, the church had run off two preachers in six months. Members had consistently refused to send any money to support denominational programs. The bishop seemed cruel to send Bessie there just before her retirement. Everyone predicted disaster.

A few months passed without my hearing a word about Bessie. Then I saw her at a denominational meeting and, fearing the worst, asked her how she was getting along at her new appointment.

"The sweetest people I have ever known!" she exclaimed. "Our first work team will leave for Brazil next month. I've got to get back early. This is our music weekend with the neighboring black congregation."

I was dumbfounded. Were we talking about the same church? What about its hatefulness? Its racism? Had there been no problems?

"Not really," replied Bessie. "There was one little misunderstanding when we voted on this year's budget."

"Misunderstanding?"

"Yes. We got to the apportionment for the black college fund. When we were about to vote on acceptance, the chairman of our board said, 'Rev. Parker, we don't give no money to that, because we ain't paying for no n*****s to go to college.'"

"That's awful! What did you do?" I asked.

"I said, 'John, that's not nice. You sit down and act like a Christian.' The whole budget passed without a single problem."

Who's going to misbehave in front of Grandmother?

Richard Baxter advised seventeenth-century Protestant pastors that "the tenderest love of a mother should not surpass ours" for our people. Bessie routinely mothered her people toward the kingdom, using any handle she could to get across the gospel—just as God used Bessie. Thank God.

The Christian Ministry,
July–August 1983

39

Embarrassment of Riches

When I heard the size of the projected budget for the coming year (I was away on vacation when the finance committee voted), I laughed. "Let me get this straight. A church that is 10 percent behind in collections for this year's budget is to have an increase of 10 percent for next year's budget? Get real!"

Still, the lay leadership persisted. (Laity are often unrealistic in their expectations.) My contribution to the fall stewardship campaign was frequently to smirk, "You'll never make that budget."

Three Sundays into the campaign, the stewardship chair made his Sunday report. "We've had something of a miracle here, folks," he said. "Just three weeks into the campaign, we have met our goal."

Spontaneous applause.

He continued, "Which is all the more amazing because next year's budget is 10 percent more than this year's."

Again, widespread applause.

"Now, as I recall, there was someone who said, when we started this venture, 'You will never make that budget.' Who was it who said that? Help me. I can't rightly remember. Who said, 'You will never make that budget'?"

"Sit down and shut up," I said, in love.

"Untimely Easter," an episcopal
sermon, July 2005

40

Pastoral Pugilism

Teaching, as I do, at a mainline Protestant seminary, I am often asked, particularly by callow seminarians, to enunciate hard-and-fast rules for pastoral work. Impressed as they are by the complex demands of the pastoral ministry, seminarians are always seeking some means of simplification. They persist in asking, "Do you think it is always wrong to perform a marriage at a nudist colony?" Others will demand, "Reverend Professor, wouldn't it always be a bad idea to use tape-recorded sound effects in a sermon?"

Alas for these meager ministerial minds, pastoral work is complex, requiring the constant exercise of mature, prudent, theologically informed pastoral judgment. After twenty years of being a pastor, I can tell you that there are few things that I would never, always, or habitually do or not do. While I cannot defend situational ethics theologically, I can certainly defend it experientially and pastorally. As a pastor, one simply must take things, and people, as they come.

For instance, I have met pastors—generally conservative traditionalists, but not always—who doggedly maintain that it is "always wrong to strike a parishioner." These tend to be the same people who feel that it is always wrong to use a comma splice within a sentence, or to begin or end a homily with the phrase, "You idiots."

Even though such sentimental, archaic notions die slowly, every pastor I know who has enjoyed more than a decade in the pastoral ministry will recall a layperson who, on one ecclesial occasion or another, has to be slugged in the jaw.

I recall, for instance, a layman of my acquaintance, a leader in one of my early congregations, who, during formal worship services, had an inclination to hum. Perhaps one hymn would remind him of another. Or perhaps, some said, he hummed as a protest against the "high church" hymn the organist and I had selected for the occasion. The hymns he hummed tended always to be evangelical ditties. A helpful layperson, seeing the dilemma that this man put me in, would nudge him with his elbow. When this failed, a particularly supportive older woman pinched him. Still, he hummed.

I was forced, as conscientious pastors often are, to take matters in hand during a Christmas Eve service last year. I found that a sharp downward blow upon his neck, smartly given, would render him into a sort of happy stupor. We had no problem with him for the remainder of the service. When he came forward for communion, he had a rather beatific smile upon his face and was most placid and receptive. He was really quite charming after that.

I know what you are thinking: A pastor who is unaware of his or her own strength could deliver a blow to a parishioner with a bit too much enthusiasm, thus helping the slugged parishioner beyond the beatific vision into lying out cold under the pew. This result is likely to prove offensive to other worshippers and, of course, ought to be avoided if at all possible. It is important not to hinder the free flow of traffic in and out of pews during a service.

Now, I have known pastors—usually those of a somewhat delicate disposition—who, to avoid overshooting the mark in striking a parishioner, would sometimes—say, during a discussion at a board meeting—merely shove the parishioner backward. They hoped thereby to achieve the needed result of silencing the offending parishioner. While restraint of force has its benefits, one of my friends, during a debate related to the annual church budget, shoved a particularly difficult man backward over a folding chair, landing him in the lap of a woman who, before that moment, had been one of the pastor's most ardent supporters. Sometimes direct, swift force is much more effective than the timid shove.

On the other hand, though a swift blow to the head—or even to the back of the neck—can be extremely effective in the long run, sometimes the affected person has a tendency to shout. While this is moderately disruptive in services of worship, it can be disastrous in church business meetings when the shout elicited thereby only serves to increase the emotional temperature of the meeting. As I have found, shouting at meetings sometimes leads to people throwing things, to others jumping on tables, and similar unfortunate side effects.

I hate to see church meetings end in a brawl as much as the next person. However, I find it surprising how even the most staid congregation will degenerate into hysterics when something is thrown during a service of worship—say, a piece of furniture, a fixture of altar ware, a hymnal, or a purse. What is there about the human species that infects it with a seemingly overwhelming desire to join in the fray once something is thrown? Undoubtedly, Calvin discussed this propensity somewhere in his *Institutes*, though I have been unable, by the date of this publication, to locate it.

Of course, everybody has, during some worship service, had the urge to throw a hymnal at someone. In my experience, this tendency is evoked most frequently by church musicians. However, interminable speakers from the Gideons, those giving sappy testimonials on "Youth Sunday," as well as representatives of the presiding bishop, also appear to have this effect upon me. While many laypersons, apathetic lot that they are, can be made to resist such a tendency, even the most jaded and morose congregation can be moved into action with a hymnal or attendance registration pad being thrown at the right moment in a service. Even the most apathetic church member or the most casual and sporadic church attender finds it difficult to sit by and do nothing, once a few hymnals are thrown at an offensive organist. This sudden burst of enthusiasm appears to be engendered not only by the excitement of sailing objects and their attendant crashes, but also by the gleeful shouts of "Gotcha!" and "How do you like that?"

Eventually, someone is bound to be knocked out cold by a poorly aimed hymnal, or a folding metal church chair improperly tossed. These things happen. It is impossible for a pastor to please everybody. My advice on these occasions is to offer apologies. Let there be consideration of whether or not the cold-cocked parishioner deserved to be knocked out cold. Then continue with the service, the meeting, or the discussion after the wounded party has been discretely dragged away.

Those who quote paragraph numbers from the *United Methodist Book of Discipline* in response to a pastor's proposal—people who, in an argument, quote from obscure passages of scripture, saying, "That may be true, Pastor, but of course you also know the advice in Obadiah, verse 4,"—earn themselves the right to be hit with a folding metal church chair. No one ever quotes scripture to a pastor without a desire to embarrass and belittle.

I also recall the man who, in a particularly difficult meeting, asked me, "Did they teach you stuff like this in seminary?" Naturally, this query begged for a sharp right thrust to the side of his jaw.

Against such pastoral care, I know of no biblical prohibition.

Thanks to James Thurber

The Door, September–October 1993

41
Who His People Are

A record of the ancestors of Jesus Christ, son of David, son of Abraham.

Matthew 1:1

In my part of the country, where family name, ancestors, and the past still count for something, an often-heard question about an unfamiliar person is, "Who were his people?" In the South we still want

to know more about where people came from than where they are going. "Who were her people?" is an inquiry into identity, an attempt to
fathom the mystery of another human being by uncovering where he or
she began.

This practice can have its negative side. "What would you have ex-
pected from someone whose people were a bunch of ex-convicts from
England?" was a Greenville matron's comment on President Jimmy
Carter's Georgia roots when he fell from favor.

Perhaps Saint Matthew spent time in Greenville. He doesn't even
call his book a Gospel, but "a record of the ancestors of Jesus Christ, son
of David, son of Abraham" (Matt 1:1). He begins with an odd genea-
logical catalog of Jesus's people: Abraham begat Isaac, Isaac begat Jacob,
Jacob begat Judah, and so on, and so on. This has to be the dullest of all
possible dull beginnings, despite all the begetting. Can you imagine trying to concoct a sermon from something so uninspiring as a genealogy?
All of our lectionaries do Matthew the favor of omitting this opening
and beginning with, "This is how the birth of Jesus Christ took place"
(Matt 1:18).

Why should we care about ancestors? Let's get on with the story
without wasting time on these patriarchs and matriarchs. And what a
curious genealogy it is! A number of those listed cannot be found anywhere in the Old Testament. They don't even rate a footnote in the
mighty acts of God. Despite Near Eastern patriarchal patterns, four
women are included, and some women they are: Tamar, who duped
poor Judah and played the whore; Rahab, the harlot of Jericho fame;
Ruth, whom we all know about; and Uriah's wife, Bathsheba, whom
David lusted after, thus producing Solomon.

It would have been helpful if Matthew had been a bit discreet and
chosen good women to mention in his list of Jesus's forebears. All of
us, if we dig far enough can find a few third cousins whom we would
rather not know, a few Tamars and Rahabs. It seems a shame to drag
such people into the story of the incarnation, to announce Jesus's birth

by bringing in women like these, or men as faulty as Isaac, Jacob and David.

Earlier, old Abram had been told, "I will make of you a great nation and will bless you. I will make your name respected, and you will be a blessing" (Gen 12:2). Here is the theological key to Matthew's biologically impossible genealogy. All of the people he lists were part of the promise to bless all of the families of God through Abraham's covenant family. All of them were part of the promise fulfilled by this baby who is called "the son of David, the son of Abraham."

Tamar, Rahab, Ruth, and Uriah's wife, for all their weaknesses or inability to fulfill the standards of conventional morality, were instruments of the promise. By sheer wit, conniving, common sense, courage, or whatever else it took, they kept the promise alive. In their willingness to be part of the covenant, these improbable saints were the forerunners of Mary, the first disciple.

Father Abraham, Isaac, Jacob, Ram, Amminadab, Nahshon, Asa, Joseph, and all the others whose names would send a Sunday school class into paroxysms of laughter—along with Tamar, Rahab, Ruth, and Uriah's wife—were all members of Jesus's family, his great-great-great granddaddies and grandmamas in the faith. For all their weaknesses and shortcomings, this motley but richly human crew were indeed his people.

You may know a lot about Jesus, Matthew seems to say. But you haven't told the whole story of this Messiah until you have told the story of Israel. This is the way God's promises are fulfilled, not by angels dropping down out of the sky, not by the saints we wish to God we were, but by people like us and our ancestors—the Tamars, Ruths, Jacobs, and Amminadabs of this world. There would be no salvation without them, without us—even them, even us.

Of course, we don't like to think this way. We spend most of our adult lives trying to detach ourselves from our stories, our families, our past, our familial peculiarities. We try to grow up and put all that behind us, leaving home, going to college, rising above mama and daddy. We want to choose the lives we lead, to be autonomous, self-made, and liberated. When we get our MAs and our sophisticated friends and our brave new world, we are embarrassed when Uncle Charlie and Aunt Agnes come to visit, lest our friends find out who our people are and where our roots lie.

But not Jesus, says Matthew. He embraces that sordid, questionable family tree, seeing himself as part of the promise made to them and through them. When he first stood in the pulpit, the congregation sneered, "Isn't that the carpenter's son? Isn't that Tamar's, Ruth's, Jacob's, Amminadab's boy?"

In Advent we wait for a Messiah who will deliver us from our humanity, from the condition that has always trapped us and traps us even now. Then, to our surprise, he comes to us the way God always does, as one of us, embracing our humanity, our history, and our hectic begetting, bidding us to become part of the promise.

We peer over the manger, asking a fitting Advent question: "Who are his people?"

Matthew answers: You know his people—Abraham, Jacob, Tamar, Ruth, and all the rest. *You* are his people.

The Christian Century,
December 14, 1983

42
Politics

My formal political instruction came by overhearing uncles' arguments during protracted Sunday dinners at my grandmother's.

"Some of the ignorantest people come from Edgefield, I tell you, Willie, and not only the Baptists," Uncle Charles pronounced in response to a request for a ruling on Edgefield-bred senator J. Strom Thurmond.

"That's the gospel truth," agreed Uncle Gene in a rare affirmation of another uncle's adjudication.

"Thieving, low-country politicians out of Barnwell ruined this state," added Uncle Henry, moving wider the geographical bounds of political ineptitude. That Henry was a lawyer and had married a Jewish woman whose family owned Greenville's biggest department store added clout to his pronouncements.

An oft-repeated political parable was of the Greenville Christmas parade when Governor Thurmond showed off by riding a huge white horse down Main Street in front of the Shriners.

Pointing to him, my cousin Rusty asked, "Who's that?"

"Don't you know?" exclaimed Uncle Gene. "That's J. Strom Thurmond."

Rusty persisted: "Who's that old man on top of J. Strom Thurmond?"

During a major political debate one Sunday at table, I ventured, "Are we going to vote for General Eisenhower?" Stunned, awkward dismay all round.

Mama maternally patted my hand. "No, dear. He is a Republican. We are Democrats." Murmurs of agreement in the assembly.

"Never met anybody with any sense in the army," added one of the uncles, "'specially the generals. Please pass the chicken. Government leeches." Consumption resumed.

"Are there Republicans around here?" I persisted.

Aggravated silence.

Mama adjusted the napkin in her lap and patiently responded, "No, dear, not that we know of."

"Well, where are Republicans?" I continued. (I had seen pictures of them on stamps in my album.)

An uncle dropped his fork, clanging into his plate, and threw up his hands. "Good Lord, God A'mighty."

"They tend to live in Illinois and Michigan, places of that nature." She sighed patiently.

"Why are they Republicans and we are Democrats?"

Those at table believed Mama had been overly indulgent. "Child, if people live by choice in places like Illinois and Michigan, they will be strange in other ways too."

"Amen," said somebody. That was that.

In college, I participated in a 1966 statewide student debate on the war in Vietnam. In response to my presentation, the dean of students at the University of South Carolina (retired army colonel) stamped and snorted, "You leftist students are ruining this country. It's unthinkable that America would lose a war!"

Upon recalling the mythmaking evasion of my white Southern family, I quipped, "Sure you can. I've got uncles who could teach you how."

First time I ran for bishop (without appearing to be running for bishop; no small feat), I withdrew on the eighth or ninth ballot. An officious layperson bustled up and said haughtily, "Reverend Willimon, I was offended by your concession speech."

"Offended?" I responded. "I withdrew! You should be pleased. I lost."

"You sounded arrogant, like you thought you were the only person who could change the Methodist Church."

"How could I be both a loser and arrogant?" I asked.

A layperson from Mississippi, standing nearby, explained, "Will's from South Carolina. Hell, his people have been both defeated and arrogant for two hundred years!"

Accidental Preacher: A Memoir, William B. Eerdmans Publishing Company, 2019

43

The Blessing of Assignment

While shaking hands with folks at the church door after service one Sunday, a person said to me, "I have had a terrible week."

"I'm sorry to hear that," I responded. (I'm such a caring pastor.)

"Trouble at work, problems at home. I came here seeking consolation and help," she said.

"Well, I hope that you found my sermon helpful," I oozed sincerely.

"Not particularly," she responded. "I came here hurting and seeking comfort only to have Jesus give me an assignment!"

How Odd of God: Chosen for the Curious Vocation of Preaching, Westminster John Knox Press, 2015

44

On the Jericho Road

While traveling home one night after a speaking engagement in a remote part of South Carolina, my car began to sputter, to falter, and finally rolled to a stop. It was ten or ten thirty on a summer evening. The stars were out, but otherwise no light could be seen anywhere. I had no idea where I was.

I got out and stood beside the car in the darkness. Five, ten minutes passed. At last, I could hear a car in the distance. I could see its lights now, and yes, here it came. I looked into its lights, smiled hopefully, as it…passed on by, barely slowing for me.

Well, at least someone is on this road tonight, I thought. But it was another fifteen minutes, a virtual eternity, before another car came. And it, too, passed by.

I got in the car, put my tie back on, straightened my hair, and resumed my post beside my stricken auto. It was late now. Who in their right mind would stop for me at midnight on a country road? Would I be stranded here all night?

Again, I saw lights coming toward me. As they came closer, I could hear music, loud music, emanating from this car. It was coming at a high rate of speed. I could tell that this car was really flying. No chance of *them* stopping. But as its lights shined in my eyes, the driver of the car put on brakes and skidded, finally coming to a stop a hundred or so feet beyond me, sliding all the way around on the pavement. Then, throwing the car into reverse, he backed up nearly as fast as he had come, screeching to a stop when he was even with my car.

I gulped. It was a multicolored old Lincoln with fender skirts, some part of some sort of animal waving from the radio antenna, and two little red, blinking lights on the back of the rearview mirror.

Oh, no, I thought. *What now? Here I am in the middle of nowhere; I'm gonna die.*

I could see two large men in the car. The one on the driver's side was wearing a T-shirt; the man on the passenger side was bare chested. He held a large can of beer and looked at me through a pair of dark glasses.

"Hey, man," he shouted at me from his window. "You got trouble?"

Now, I've got trouble. "I'm just resting, counting stars, letting my engine cool; don't trouble yourself over me."

Before I could say anything else, these strangers were out of their car, had my hood up, offered me refreshments, and were tinkering with my motor. Nearly an hour later, long after a dozen other cars had passed by on the other side, with the moon well on its way down the western sky, the two shook my hand, bid me farewell with, "Take it easy, neighbor," and squealed off into the darkness of a low country summer night. I headed home.

A Samaritan, who was on a journey, came to where the man was. But when he saw him, he was moved with compassion. (Luke 10:33)

"On the Jericho Road," sermon, Trinity
United Methodist Church, September 15, 1974

45

Fathers and Sons Needed Deliverance from the River

"Yes sir, Mr. Williston, nothing brings a father and son together like a canoe trip," said the man at the canoe rental store.

"That's Willimon," I countered.

"Whatever," he replied. "Like I was saying, something happens to father to son when you're out in open water, stroking your way down some peaceful river. We can give you everything you need right here, Mr. Williamson."

"That's Willimon, and I already know something about canoeing. I once earned my canoeing merit badge in Boy Scouts."

This information did not seem to impress the canoe rental man. "That was a while ago, I take it," he said.

"Well, yes, but I still know how to do a mean J-stroke," I said, slightly offended.

"The main thing is for you to pick a good, slow, undemanding river. I've got just the river for you—the Cape Fear."

"If it's so good, why do they call it Fear?" I asked.

"You Duke professors are all alike," he said, laughing to himself.

The trip seemed the right thing to do, at least that's what Charles Putman thought. He would take a couple of days away from the medical center. I would take time away from the chapel, and we would take our sons, aged twelve and eleven, on the great Cape Fear for an adventure. Just the thing to bring fathers and sons close together.

We left Durham one hot August day, bound for Fuquay–Varina with two canoes strapped on my station wagon. We would've arrived in the river earlier and that would have helped, but Charles insisted that we stop for extra supplies. He emerged from Watson's Grocery with a package of doughnuts, two cans of Vienna sausage, about 100 feet of twine, a set of rubber gloves, a long kitchen knife, and a sun visor.

I ask him what he intended to do with twine.

At last we reached the place on the Cape Fear River where we had been instructed, by the canoe rental man, to put in our canoes. "They've improved these canoes, since you was a kid," the man at the rental place and told me. "Now they are real light."

After we had taken them off the top of our car and loaded the canoes down to the water, I wasn't so sure. The fathers had to do all the loading of the canoes, since they were too heavy for the boys to lift.

"This is called 'portage,'" explained Charles.

"This is called heavy," said I, "very heavy."

Within an hour, our canoes were in the water, loaded with gear, and we were headed down the mighty Cape Fear.

"Dad, you think we ought to wrap the plastic around our gear, so it won't get wet?" one of the boys asked.

"No," both of the dads replied.

"No chance of our stuff getting wet because we know what we're doing and we are not going to turn the canoes over. I have my canoeing merit badge," said I.

"That was a long time ago," said the sons.

"Besides the last thing the weatherman said was no chance of rain for the next couple of days," added Charles.

So, we paddled ahead, singing the first verse of "Alouette." We had sung the first verse over about a thousand times and had been paddling for about twenty minutes when one of the boys said, "I think I hear thunder."

We both repeated to them what the weatherman had said.

A few minutes later, we all heard thunder. The sky toward the south appeared to be the color of fresh asphalt.

"Maybe we better head into the bank until this blows over," we agreed.

Before we got to the bank, the rain had begun. By the time we finally got the canoes tied to a tree and we were on the bank, it was raining in buckets. The thunder grew increasingly loud. It was pouring now. We stood on the bank and watched our canoes slowly fill with water until both of them sank.

"I doubt wrapping the gear and plastic would've helped anyway," said one of the sons, attempting to make us feel better.

The thunder grew louder. The boys seemed anxious. Never one to miss an opportunity to educate the young, I told the boys as the rain continued to soak us, "You can calculate how close the lightning is by counting from the time you see the flash until the moment you hear the thunder. The speed of light versus the speed of sound. Let's try it." Just then there was this incredible ball of fire over us, immediately followed by the loudest *Bam!* I ever heard.

"I calculate that the lightning is about ten inches from us," said Charles. "That's by calculating raw fear with unrelenting terror."

"You think we ought to stop calculating and start saying the Lord's Prayer?" asked his son.

"I've already tried it," said my son. "It doesn't work."

The thunder crashed. A huge limb fell from a tree near us and splashed into the river. It was as dark as night. The rain was pouring so hard that we could neither see the river nor shout above the roar.

But after an eternity, it was over. We were wet, cold, miserable, but grateful to be alive. By the time we had bailed all the water out of the canoes, it was nearly night. We decided to revise our plans; paddle all the way back up the river, from whence we had come; load the canoes back on the car, along with the gear; and drive to the state park where we were to spend the night, rather than risk paddling down the river to the park in darkness and high water.

By the time we got to the park, it was almost eight o'clock. The ranger told us that the canoe campsite was "a relatively short walk, no more than a mile from the parking lot." Each father took a canoe and hoisted it on his back. The boys each loaded themselves with our wet, soggy gear, and we slipped and slid down the muddy trail to the canoe campsite. A mile is a relatively long walk with the canoe on your back.

Once there, we found that the campsite had no electricity or water and that it was an utterly miserable place to roll out our wet sleeping bags. Besides, the boys had forgotten to bring the tent.

Resigned, each of the fathers took a canoe, hoisted it on his back, the boys each loaded themselves with our now more wet, soggy gear, and we slipped and slid back up the winding trail to the parking lot. We dumped our equipment at the edge of the parking lot and drove into Lillington to eat our evening meal at Hardee's. It wasn't sitting around the campfire, roasting hot dogs and singing songs, as we had planned, but it was nourishment.

By the time we got back to the state park, the gate was closed for the night. We abandoned our car outside the gate and walked in a mile or so to the parking lot.

"My only regret," said Charles as we walked in the darkness, "is that I don't have a canoe on my back. Lovely night for a damn walk."

We put down a tarp at the parking lot, though I don't know why, unrolled our soggy sleeping bags, and prepared to spend the night.

No sooner had we crawled into our wet beds than I was blinded by a flashlight, shining in my eyes.

"Sir, it is my duty, as a duly authorized park officer of the State of North Carolina, to tell you that you are now camping in an un-designated area. You will have to remove your sleeping bags, pick up your canoes, and move. I will have to fine you fifty dollars each for this violation."

In the eerie glow of the flashlight, I could see Charles's eyes glisten-ing in a frightening way. I was afraid that he might have reached the breaking point, that he might crack under pressure, that this last event might've brought him to the end of his rope, or twine. I couldn't forget that Charles was originally from Texas.

"Officer," I said, "I know we don't look like it right at this moment, but we are two very influential people back at Duke University, where we work. I am the university minister and this man has a very high-paid job at the medical center. Now, if you allow us to leave our tents and ca-noes here, just for the night, I'm prepared to offer you a free wedding or funeral for the relative of your choice, and Dr. Putman will arrange for a hysterectomy or an appendectomy, free of charge at the Duke Medical Center."

The park ranger stepped back a couple of paces. "Look," he said, pleading, "I don't want no trouble. They don't allow us to carry firearms. If you will get out of here by daybreak, I'll let you stay."

We thanked him. He quickly left. It was nearly midnight. The sleeping bags were soaked. Charles realized that he had left his pipe tobacco back at Hardee's in Lillington. It was the end of the first day of the Great Father-Son Canoe Adventure, now redesignated as "Canoes to Hell and Back."

The next morning, we arose at dawn and feasted on soggy donuts and two cans of Vienna sausages. Charles and I hoisted the canoes on our backs and carried them back down to the river. By now we figured that we had carried the canoes for a total of four miles, longer than we had paddled the canoes on our first day on the Cape Fear.

"I know fathers who couldn't have done this," I said to the boys proudly. "Thank the Lord. I once participated in a three-month exercise research project at the medical center. It was a long time ago, but I think it prepared me."

"If we ever get out of this alive," Charles muttered (with no indication that he thought we ever would), "I intend to lift and carry a canoe at least once every day to keep myself in shape."

I was really beginning to worry about Charles's emotional stability. I couldn't get off my mind that originally he was from Texas.

"I tell you, the worst is over," I pronounced. "From here on out, it's just lie back and float down the Cape Fear."

"What do we do if we hit some rapids?" my son asked.

"Then we just grit our teeth and take them head-on," I said.

As it turns out, there aren't any rapids on the Cape Fear. About ten miles above Lillington, the Cape Fear turns into the consistency of Jell-O. The whole river comes to a dead stop. This means that, if you want to go down the Cape Fear, you've got to paddle every inch of the way. The canoes move down the river with all the ease and grace of Brillo pads being rubbed against sandpaper.

The sun was hot. Large, cannibalistic bugs had found us. We tried sitting while we paddled, kneeling while we paddled; nothing made it easier. For seven hours we paddled. And you know who did most of the paddling.

By three o'clock, we sighted a railroad trestle, only a hundred yards away, a sign of Lillington. Columbus, seeing land at the end of his first voyage, couldn't have been happier than the four of us. We paddled now for everything we were worth.

It was another hour before we were in Lillington.

We struggled to pull the canoes up the high bank where we had left our car.

"I don't think I have the energy to lift the canoes up on top of the car," I groaned.

"Sure, you do," said Charles. "I love lifting them. I hope we can lift them about eight more times. I will carry them around all over the streets of Lillington!" he screamed.

I was beginning to wonder if Charles would ever recover from the trip.

At last the canoes were on top of the car, tied down securely. We got in the car, turned the ignition. The car would not start.

"Boys, get out of the car," I said.

"Why?" they asked.

"Because I don't want to see a grown man cry," I said.

Charles was now whimpering like a baby.

We pulled ourselves together, got out of the stalled car, and trudged up the embankment, out to the highway into Lillington, and plodded toward town. Fortunately, the Chevrolet dealership is on the edge of town. We stopped there, even though my car is a Nissan. We were greeted amiably by a man, shoes and socks off, leaning backward in a chair against the wall.

"How you boys?" the man asked. "What brings you to town?"

Charles and I looked really bad. We had not shaved in forty-eight hours. We were wet and sunburned. "Sir," I said, "we've been on the Cape Fear River. We've had some car trouble, and I need to call Durham for help."

"Sure. Use my phone, for free," he said. "Just goes to show, don't it?"

"Goes to show what?" Charles said.

"Goes to show that you boys shouldn't have been off having a good time fishing on that river. If you had been like me, working, like you were supposed to be, then you wouldn't be in this fix, right?"

"Charles, you wait outside," I ordered.

I called for help from Durham. We unloaded the canoes off my car, loaded them onto Charles's truck, tied them down, then drove back to Durham.

"Can we do this again next summer?" asked my son. "I'd like to follow the Cape Fear all the way to Wilmington."

"You really need to do something about that kid," said Charles.

It was now black, dark, the second day of our adventure. As the boys slept peacefully in the back of the truck, we unloaded the canoes one last time at the lot of the rental place.

"Just for old time's sake," said Charles, "let's load them on the truck once more." I didn't answer him. I was on my way back home for a shower.

That evening, at the end of the divinity school faculty dinner (where I arrived two hours late), the dean looked at me and said, in a sarcastic tone, "I can see that it was too much for us to have expected you here this evening. You're obviously worn-out from having been on the golf course all day."

I am a person of restraint. Without a word, I turned the other cheek and left.

A few weeks after what became known as the Great Father-Son-Canoe Cape Fear Adventure, I was standing in line at the opening convocation with Dean Malcolm Gillis of the graduate school. Dean Gillis was complaining about something Dr. Charles Putman had said to him after a meeting.

"Go easy on Charles this year," I said. "The man has come very close to death. That can affect a person's emotions. Besides that, he's from Texas. We're all going to have to be real patient with him for awhile."

Nothing brings people together—fathers and sons, doctors and preachers—like being face-to-face with mortality. When you get a chance, take a canoe trip down the Cape Fear. You'll know what I mean.

Charles will be happy to help you with the canoes.

Duke Dialogue, September 1987

46
—
Vocative God

At the Northside UMC Wednesday morning prayer breakfast (God and a sausage biscuit at an ungodly hour), I piously asked the assembled laity, hoping to impress them with the earnestness of my pastoral care, "Pray for Mary. Johnny was booked last night. DUI. I'm going to see what I can do to get him out. Mary's had a time with that boy."

"How much you know about alcoholism?" said one of the men, unimpressed by my ministry.

"Where you going to get the money for bail?" asked another. "We'll go with you. Take this off the prayer list. We can handle it."

The three of us walked into the bowels of the jail, where we saw a frightened youth, huddled in the corner of a cell, weeping.

"Son, how long have you had a problem with alcohol?" one of the men asked through the bars.

"Uh, I wouldn't say I have a 'problem,'" Johnny replied.

"Let me rephrase that. How long have you been lying about your problem with alcohol? Son, I've learned a lot about booze the hard way. Had that monkey on my back since I was in the army. I can show you the way out."

"We're springing you," said another, who was a lawyer. "And you come home with me. Our kids are out of the house. Your mama's got enough on her already. I'd love to have somebody to watch Clemson football with."

A vocative God showing off.

Accidental Preacher: A Memoir, William
B. Eerdmans Publishing Company, 2019

47
Savior

I once knew a woman who was assaulted in broad daylight in her backyard. It was horrible. We got her a great counselor who specializes in such violent tragedies. One day she said, "My counselor wants me to tell my story to someone who is not a member of my family, as a therapeutic help."

"Have you thought of someone?" I asked.

"Yes. I'd like to tell Harry Jones," she said. Harry Jones was a sometimes-recovering, often not, always unemployed alcoholic.

"Why Harry?" I asked. "I thought you might want to tell another woman."

"Why Harry? Because he knows what it's like to go to hell," she replied, "and still make it back."

And I thought: *Only in the church would someone whom the world despises and regards as a failure be your savior.*

"On the Jericho Road," sermon, Trinity
United Methodist Church, September 15, 1974

48
Two People at Prayer

It was Saturday night. There was a knock at my door. I opened the door to find a policeman standing on my doorstep.

"Preacher," he said, "could you come with me? Some of your church members have gotten into a big brawl and the chief thinks you might be able to help us settle them down."

Some of my *church* members. How could this be?

"Now, cut out that shooting, Joe, and you two settle down and come on out. You're going to hurt somebody if you ain't careful," blared the chief's voice across the debris-strewn yard. I could see broken glass and overturned furniture, some inside, some outside of the house. It was an apocalyptic vision of chaos and battle. Another shot rang out from the house and the chief ducked back down behind his car.

This is no place for a man of the cloth, I thought, as I inched my way over to the chief's car.

"How are you doing, Reverend?" the chief asked amicably as I joined him in his improvised bunker.

"Not all that well at the moment," I replied.

"Joe and his wife are having a little argument, it seems. It has gotten a bit rough and we thought that maybe you could help us settle them down," said the chief.

"A little argument?"

"Yes, they usually have one of these every spring."

"You mean to tell me this has happened before?" I asked with quivering voice.

"Oh sure, it's not all that big a deal. They just seem to let things build up during the winter, and then every spring they let it all out, so to speak."

And to think, one of my "best" church members.

No shots or curses came from the house for five or ten minutes and, after repeated attempts by the chief to elicit some response from Joe or his wife, the chief pronounced, "They have probably passed out now. It's safe to go on in and get them."

I accompanied the police into the scene of the heart of battle (at a safe distance), where we found Joe and his wife, just as the chief had predicted, passed out on their living room sofa, a bit bruised, scratched up here and there, but apparently in surprisingly good condition for two battle-weary veterans. By that time, neighbors had arrived and were clearing away the debris and helping the two groggy combatants into bed. The chief led his men back to their cars, saying something about, "Well, that ought to hold them until this time next year."

As for me, I was shocked, disappointed, angry, but mainly I was embarrassed. I returned home determined to relieve Joe of his church duties as soon as possible. Was this any way for one of my members to act?

The next morning, in the quietness and beauty of church, the disorder of the evening seemed far away. As I moved through the worship service, I had hardly given the episode a thought until we came to the offering. I dutifully got the offering plates and turned to hand them to the head usher. And who should be the head usher on this Sunday? Joe. I nearly passed out when I turned around and saw him standing there, smiling sheepishly, bandages on his bruised hands and a cut under one eye, more or less reverently waiting for the plates; Joe, standing there before me, God, and everybody else. This was more than I could take. The nerve of the man. Had he no pride? No self-respect? Can you imagine someone having the nerve to stand up before the altar on Sunday morning after a Saturday night like that?

He had no pride?

Jesus told this parable to certain people who had convinced themselves that they were righteous and who looked on everyone else with disgust: "Two people went up to the temple to pray. One was a Pharisee and the other a tax collector. The Pharisee stood and prayed about himself with these words, 'God, I thank you that I'm not like everyone else— crooks, evildoers, adulterers—or even like this tax collector. I fast twice a week. I give a tenth of everything I receive.' But the tax collector stood at a distance. He wouldn't even lift his eyes to look toward heaven. Rather, he struck his chest and said, 'God, show mercy to me, a sinner.' I tell you, this person went down to his home justified rather than the Pharisee." (Luke 18:9-14)

"Pharisees and Publicans All," sermon,
Duke University Chapel, October 26, 1986

Part Three

Senses

This people's senses have become calloused...
Everyone who has ears should pay attention...
You will hear but never understand...
Although they see, they don't really see...
Happy eyes; happy ears...

49

Come, Join the Party

I checked in at the hotel about five on Saturday evening. Only a few finishing touches needed before I could put my sermon to bed for Sunday morning. Presbyterians. One of the oldest churches in town. Brought my black robe to lend gravitas to my demeanor. Presbyterians eat up gravitas.

As I went down the hall toward my room, fumbling with my plastic key card, checking the room number, I bumped into a man coming out of his room, ice bucket in hand.

"Hey buddy, George Walker here." He thrust his free hand toward me with a wide grin.

"Will," I said.

"Look, glad I ran into you. Some of the boys are in town and we're throwing a helluva party tonight. Got some great girls coming over. One of 'em a Miss South Carolina runner-up couple of years ago."

"Thank you," I said, formally.

"Don't need to bring a thing. We got drinks for everybody," he shouted as he walked down toward the ice and vending.

"But I actually have an early appointment tomorrow," I called. "Thanks anyway."

He didn't seem to hear me over his whistling.

I had dinner with my hosts that evening, members of the Session. When I returned to the hotel around nine, I could hear music, loud music, the moment I stepped out of the elevator. Pulsating from my new friend's room.

Thank the Lord I'm an experienced traveler who's got ear plugs.

As providence would have it, George's door opened just as I walked by. "Hey! William, Bill, was afraid you wouldn't make it. Come on, we're just getting started!"

I explained to George, as best I could over the music, that I had an early morning tomorrow, Sunday, the Lord's Day, and couldn't come to the party.

"Aw, come on. You don't have to stay all night. Got a great bunch of people for you to meet."

"Thanks, but I really can't come to your party," I said, pleasantly but firmly.

"You're going to be sorrrrry," George said with a grin as he returned to the party.

I prepared for bed, carefully setting out the earplugs. But before I could get into bed, there was a startling knock at my door.

It was George. "Billy, I just can't let you miss out on this," he said. "Come on, just a few minutes? Charlene has brought some of her girlfriends and—"

"George," I said in as mature a voice as I could muster, standing behind the door in my underwear, "I'm not coming to the party. That's it. Good night."

I shut the door and went to sleep, fitfully.

The next morning, on my way down the hall, black robe over my arm, Bible in hand, out comes bleary-eyed-but-still-smiling George. "Bill, missed one helluva party, that's all I got to say."

A woman's voice in the room said, "Georgie, come on back, honey."

George sighed and shut the door.

Here's my point. That was thirty years ago. I've preached at many great churches since then, published a few books, been a bishop. I've been to some great places and had some wonderful experiences. And yet... *I still wish I had gone to that party.*

See Matthew 22:1-14.

"The Judgment of Grace," sermon,
Battelle Chapel, Yale University,
October 9, 2011

50
Good Friday

Really now, Lord Jesus, is our sin so serious as to necessitate the sort of ugly drama we are forced to behold this day? Why should the noon sky turn toward midnight and the earth heave and the heavens be rent for our mere peccadilloes? To be sure, we've made our mistakes. Things didn't turn out as we intended. There were unforeseen complications, factors beyond our control. But we meant well. We didn't intend for anyone to get hurt. We're only human, and is that so wrong?

Really now, Lamb of God who takes away the sins of the world, we may not be the very best people who ever lived, but surely we are not the worst. Others have committed more serious wrong. Ought we to be held responsible for the ignorance of our grandparents? They, like we, were doing the best they could, within the parameters of their time and place. We've always been forced to work with limited information. We suffer a huge gap between our intentions and our results.

Please, Lord Jesus, die for someone else, someone whose sin is more spectacular, more deserving of such supreme sacrifice. We don't want the responsibility.

Really, Lord, is our unrighteousness so very serious? Are we such sinners that you should need to die for us?

Really, if you look at the larger picture, our sin, at least my sin, is so inconsequential. You are making too big a deal out of my meager rebellion. We don't want your blood on our hands. We don't want our lives to bear the burden of your death. Really. Amen.

Why Jesus?, Abingdon Press, 2010

51
Confirmed

When I was ten, my mother deposited me at Buncombe Street Methodist (founded long before H. L. Mencken invented "bunkum") every Thursday afternoon for the church membership class. I retained nothing about Methodism from that class. My confirmation occurred not in the church sanctuary on a Sunday but rather in the parking lot on Thursday before Holy Week. On Palm Sunday we were to be joined to the church. The bulletin that Sunday was to feature a photo of the class lined up on the steps in front of the Ionic columns of Buncombe Street. (The facade earned the church a nickname, Jesus First National Bank.)

Thursday, I was greeted by the woman who commanded the confirmands: "Where's your tie?"

I froze.

"You were told to wear a tie. We're taking the confirmands' photo. There's a photographer—*a professional*. Dr. Herbert is to have his picture taken with the class—*the preacher*."

She waved her hand over the assembled righteous. "Every boy has a tie. Even Stanley Starnes. See? You were told."

Words failed. I wheeled around and dashed out the door to the back parking lot. I would post myself at the preacher's parking space, head him off, confess my sin, and humbly bow out of the picture.

Sure enough, there was Dr. Herbert, pulling his light blue Plymouth into the space. I breathlessly ran up and blurted, "Dr. Herbert, you don't know me, but I'm William Willimon, and I didn't hear that we were supposed to have a tie, or I forgot, or maybe my mother didn't tell me, and I don't want to be in the picture anyway, and…"

Dr. Herbert, with his stained-glass bass voice, replied, "Tie? Why on earth would you be wearing a tie? I am wearing a tie because I'm a pastor and I am forced to wear a tie. I'm unaware that you have had theological training."

All I've had is this dumb class.

"Are you not preparing yourself for membership in the Methodist Church?" he continued.

"Yessir."

"Well, son, I know more about these matters than anyone present, and I'm certain that there are no requirements in Methodism for ties to be worn in order to join the church. No record of our Lord ever having worn a tie, and I know Scripture. Come along. The whole point of these ceremonials is to put you in the picture."

He led me back into the darkened hall toward the primary classroom, where the others were detained.

"Everyone's here," reported the woman in charge. "Nearly everyone has dressed for the photograph, as they were told. Even Stanley Starnes."

My heart stopped.

"What a beautiful group!" exclaimed Dr. Herbert. "I have but one request before we go out and take our place on the church steps. Boys, please, no ties on a Thursday. Only I can wear a tie in church on a weekday. Such are the rules of our connection. You may wear them if you must on Sunday. Please remove your ties. Let's take that picture."

God is like Dr. Herbert, without the Plymouth.

Accidental Preacher: A Memoir, William
B. Eerdmans Publishing Company, 2019

52

Jews and Christians, All in the Family

Luke told a story about a troubled family in which a younger son, after a lurid sojourn, returned home in rags and smelling of the cheap perfume of harlots. The waiting father received him with joy. A party began. But the older brother—working for the father—refused to go to the party. The father came out into the darkness and pleaded with the brother to come in (Luke 15:1-32).

In our day, in the relationship of Christians and Jews, the story has taken a sad and unexpected turn, one that Luke couldn't have imagined. The younger brother soon lost his repentant, contrite spirit. The shock of his father's gracious reception wore off. He came to resent his older brother's failure to party at his homecoming. He began to scheme against his brother, to take on airs, to forget how fortunate he was to be in his Father's house. At last he even resorted to locking the older brother out of the house. He bolted the door, and the party, which had been a celebration for the reception of a stranger, became the victory bash of the arrogant usurper.

The music and dancing resumed. The smug younger brother had it all to himself now. But outside, in the December darkness, stood the father, where he had left him, standing where he had always been, beside the older brother.

The younger brother had succeeded in locking out his brother, he had the whole house to himself, but, alas, he had locked out his loving father as well.

"Jews and Christians, All in the Family,"
sermon, Duke University Chapel,
December 7, 1986

53
Contextual Preaching

"So, are you taking any preaching classes?" Mr. Parker (my soon-to-be father-in-law) asked.

"Yes sir."

"Good," he said.

I thought I'd flatter the Reverend Parker by asking him a question about preaching, since he had been in the business for four decades.

"Have you any advice to offer a budding preacher from your many years of experience in the pulpit? What's the most important thing I can do to preach well?"

After a moment's thought Mr. Parker said, "Context. Preaching is so very context-dependent. A good sermon is the word of God, yes, but always applied to a specific people in a specific time and place."

"How do I make sure that my sermons are appropriately contextual?" I asked, figuring that he would enjoy giving me fatherly advice.

"Son, begin by finding out where they are. Don't assume anything. Discover what sort of faith formation they've had. Take my first congregation. Fresh out of Duke Divinity School in 1938, the bishop sent me to the most God-forsaken church in South Carolina, down near Aynor. Backward, let me tell you. Benighted! Lord have mercy.

"So, at my first meeting I asked them some questions so I'd know just what I was facing. 'How many of you have ever heard of John Wesley?' They sat there staring back at me. A couple of old farmers shrugged their shoulders, ignorant as they could be of our Wesleyan heritage.

"*Humph.* 'Well, how many of you have ever heard of Jesus Christ?' Again, blank stares.

"*My Lord!* 'Look, how many of you have ever heard of God?' They gaped, stared at the ceiling, shrugged their shoulders. Finally, one old man asked, 'Preacher, is his last name Damnit?'"

54

Inspired Preaching

How I loved Birmingham's Church of the Reconciler—church for, by, and with the homeless. The first time I preached at Church of the Rec, after the call to worship, I gazed at the gathering gleaned off the city streets and realized that my proposed sermon was a stupid mistake. I tossed my sermon and prayed, "Come on, Lord, give me something. I'm dying down here. You owe me. Line!" That frantic prayer, though prayed often, has rarely been answered—the Lord builds character by having a preacher publicly experience being "poor in spirit." But that day, with a congregation of the wretched of the streets before me, the Holy Spirit fed me the words.

"It's always a blessing to be with you," I began. "Now the question for this morning is: What did Jesus do for a living? What line of work was he in?"

Silence. Finally, someone ventured, "Carpentry?"

"Good guess. No. His daddy, Joseph, was a carpenter, but no record of Jesus ever helping out in the shop."

"A preacher?" tried another.

"Right! But back then, people didn't yet know that you could de-fang a preacher with a good salary and a fat pension. No, Jesus couldn't have earned a living wage by preaching."

"Did Jesus have an apartment?" somebody called out.

"Great question!" I said. "Nothing about Jesus working, but we do know that 'even foxes had holes to crawl into at night but the Son of Man had nowhere to lay his head.' Homeless, he was. Here's the truth: Jesus Christ was an unemployed, homeless beggar... That's why he accepted so many dinner invitations, even to homes where he wasn't liked. He was hungry and had nowhere else to go."

Somebody down front shouted, "That's all right, Jesus! I ain't got no job neither! That's all right!" Applause in the congregation.

"That's all right!"

"No job, no house, no nothin', just like Jesus!" shouted a woman who danced in the aisle as the band struck up. General applause and adoration from the assembly.

A few raucous minutes later, I waved the congregation to silence. "You've got my drift. Christians believe that a homeless [*drum roll*], jobless [*"Amen!"*] Jew [*"Go ahead!"*] is the whole truth about who God is and what God is up to.

"So," I shouted above the joyful din, "that means that even with degrees from Yale and Emory, even though I can read this stuff in Greek, some of you are closer to Jesus than your bishop!"

Dancing and shouting resumed.

Accidental Preacher: A Memoir, William
B. Eerdmans Publishing Company, 2019

55
Relentless Pursuit

My first comments, in the first five minutes of the first class, were these: "Students, this is a high-level, rather complicated philosophy class with demanding material. I want you all to do well on the final exam. I want everyone in the class to get an A. I urge you to begin reading immediately and don't fall behind. I want everyone to do well."

After class, she told me, "I'm just not good at this philosophy stuff. Maybe I ought to drop the class."

"Don't do that! You haven't had philosophy with me. I'm sure you will do fine, and, if you run into trouble, I'm willing to help. I want everyone to do well."

Sure enough, just as she said, she wasn't much of a philosopher. She flunked the midterm.

"Don't get discouraged," I told her after that class. "I want to help you. I'm willing to meet with you every week and personally help you succeed in this course. How are Thursdays for you, two to four?"

She reluctantly agreed. That Thursday, I was in my office waiting on her for our tutorial. She didn't show. Next class I said to her, "What happened Thursday? Remember, I'm here for you and want to help you ace this class." She made some lame excuse about Thursdays being the only day she could get her washing done, something like that.

"See you next week, Thursday, two to four," I said as she left.

Next Thursday I sat in my office, alone.

I kept bugging her after each class, "Nearly at the end of the semester. Need to get busy. If Thursdays are not good for you, with your wash and everything, pick another day that would work."

Nothing. End of the semester, last class, I could tell she was clueless. "It's the midnight hour," I said to her. "I'll block out all of Tuesday for us to meet and I'll personally give you all you need to know to do well on the exam. How's Tuesday for you?"

She agreed, sort of.

All day Tuesday I sat there. No show.

So, the afternoon before the exam, I find out where she lives and I go there. One of those young adult party/apartment complexes the students love. I ring her doorbell. No answer. So, I wait in my car, watching. At five she rolls in the lot. I watch her go up the steps to her apartment with this random guy in tow. Before I could make my move, she and this guy race out together, holding hands, jump into his car, and screech out of the lot.

Well, I follow them. As I could have predicted, they head toward the Green Lizard, a favorite student hangout. I watch as they go inside. I wait to make my move. Then, in a few minutes, I go in and immediately spy them gyrating on the dance floor. I come up to them and I say to her, "Hey! Didn't we have an exam study session today? I guess you thought you'd get away without attending!"

Her date tried to intervene, so I said, "Back off kid. She's my student. Don't want to see you get hurt. Nothing stands in my way when I'm helping her get an A in my class."

So, I lead her out. She gets in my car, and I take her back to her place.

"Put on a pot of coffee. We've got a long night ahead," I tell her. I sit at her kitchen table and, beginning with the first class, I spoon-feed her the entire course.

Around midnight she moans, "I just can't take any more of this. Can't keep my eyes open."

I tell her to go to bed. I'll stay here on the sofa and we can finish the review first thing tomorrow.

At six I put on the coffee and knock on her bedroom door, saying cheerfully, "Rise and shine! Today's the day you show you are good in philosophy!"

By nine, I walk her into the classroom. Exams are distributed, and I can tell, just watching her sail through the questions, that she is on her way to an A.

Now, I didn't do that. To conduct myself in that manner would be highly unprofessional if not downright illegal. No principled professor would do that.

But God does.

See Matthew 20:1-9.

"The Invitation," a sermon, preached
too many times and too many places.

56
Theological Test

Bishop Tullis, speaking to a group of us soon-to-be ordained, urging us to prepare ourselves well for ministry, recalled a Kentucky preacher, pastor of a tall-steeple church, who took a few days off for deer hunting in the mountains.

Third day in the bush, the preacher started back to his car, but he couldn't find where he had parked it. He wandered in the woods for a couple of hours; then, in desperation as darkness fell, he fired his gun, hoping to attract someone's attention.

No sooner had he fired his gun than a game warden stepped out of the brush, saying, "I'm fining you for hunting at night."

The preacher told him, "I wasn't hunting. I was trying to get help. Besides, I'm a law-abiding Methodist preacher in Louisville."

The game warden looked suspiciously at the scruffy man before him with a three-day growth of beard. Nothing about him looked clerical.

"If you are really a Methodist preacher, let me hear you say the Lord's Prayer," said the warden.

The preacher, who was discombobulated by his plight, began, "The Lord is my shepherd. I shall not want. He maketh me to lie down in green—"

"By God, you are a Methodist preacher!" exclaimed the warden.

57
An Ordinary Passover

Those of us who are students of these popular Near Eastern religious movements find little of note in him, his teaching, his origin or his ending; typical. The fuss over his death is hardly justified by the ascertainable facts: He came from common stock. Son of a carpenter. Mother, ordinary. Certainly nothing in his background or family to distinguish him from your standard Galilean. Never traveled outside Judea or availed himself of classical, higher education. Some sort of scandal related to his birth, I hear. Nothing in his childhood or youth of note.

And so, it was surprising to find him—despite his relative youth, inexperience, and lack of training—teaching and interpreting, assuming titles, gathering disciples. He read well enough when he presided at Nazareth, but his sermon, we are told, was a left-wing exaggeration of Isaiah's messianism. His style bordered on the vain and egotistical. Nazareth was unimpressed by his preaching. Sent him packing, they say. I could find no one in his hometown who speaks well of him. "Joe and Mary's boy, isn't he?" they responded.

His reputation was made elsewhere. Over in Capernaum, he became something of a celebrity. A large crowd followed him about, especially the women, commoners on the whole. He entertained them with your usual healings, exorcisms, water-into-wine, multiplication of loaves, and other tricks.

Nothing of note, nothing spectacular. But the people loved it. Claudius tells me that he has had more than a couple of these indigenous messiahs over in Syria.

His teaching? Undistinguished. Some simplistic and hackneyed clichés from the rabbis, proof-texting that rehashed their prophets—certainly nothing original. Cleverly arranged at times, but we've heard it all before. He was in no way an original thinker, theologically speaking. He packaged it well, and managed to speak with authority. A great many of the unlettered malcontents were intrigued to the point of fanaticism—the type of irrational fervor one often observes among the poor. Some left their trades and roved about the countryside with him, calling him "Rabbi" and making all sorts of extravagant claims for him. But that is to be expected.

So far as I know, this was his first foray into Jerusalem. He had wisely avoided the big cities, heretofore, undoubtedly realizing that his support lay in the hinterland.

He took Jerusalem by storm last week when he arrived, which surprised me. Pilgrims from the outlying districts were here, raising a great commotion as he entered, having been worked up to a frenzy by his advance men. But the city proved to be his undoing. By the end of the week, his indiscretion was apparent. The people soon grew tired of him, as they often do in these cases. Official Jerusalem was, on the whole, unimpressed.

I was forced to step in and take matters in hand when it appeared there would be civil unrest unless he and his followers were contained. I know, I know; there is bound to be criticism by outsiders, and some bleeding hearts will cry injustice. But he was shown due process in my interrogations. The law was honored to the letter, though it was a great waste of my time. It was all quite open and aboveboard.

So far as I can discover, these are the basics of my report. The facts from reliable sources. All in all, it has been a rather uneventful week here in Jerusalem; your typical Passover. A fitting end to the life of a rather ordinary man.

This case is closed.

The Christian Century, March 5, 1980

58

Say It

While courting Patsy, I attended church with her family one Sunday. I was nervous because, unlike the Parkers, my family took church in small doses. Mr. Parker was then serving as the Marion district superintendent. We paraded like ducks behind Mr. Parker from the district parsonage to beige-bricked First Methodist Church. I had been warned that Carl Parker was miserable being consigned to a pew, forced to listen to another preach. The church's sad little pastor appeared to be jittery about preaching to the DS and his family, plus the boyfriend.

"We need to be more committed to Christ!" he said, hastily adding, "I don't mean to the point of fanaticism, or to the neglect of family responsibilities. We are not Baptists, after all." He guffawed apprehensively. None in the congregation returned his laugh.

"We must be more involved in the church, though many of you lead busy lives and sometimes it's just impossible to be present... I pray for a rebirth of good old Methodist piety, but not the showy sort. Nobody likes religion worn on the sleeve."

Bunyan's "Mr. Facing-Both-Ways" ricocheted on, one retrieval after another, with Carl Parker exaggeratedly, repeatedly pulling out his railroad pocket watch that some congregation had gifted him, looking at the time, shaking his head, and thrusting it back in his vest pocket with an audible sigh.

After the sermon finally rolled over and died, we paraded out, Mr. Parker barely acknowledging the preacher. We walked single file back to the district parsonage. Preacher Parker slung open the front door and stomped up the stairs toward his bedroom, ripping off his tie. On his way up he wheeled on the landing, seething, shaking his finger at me. "Boy, let me tell you one thing. If God should call you into the ministry, and if you go to seminary..."

"Yes sir?"

"And if you are ordained, and if the bishop entrusts you with a congregation, and if God gives you something to say, *for God's sake, would you say it!*"

Accidental Preacher: A Memoir, William
B. Eerdmans Publishing Company, 2019

59

When Does a Sermon Begin?

Monday

So, I tried too much yesterday. Is that a sin? This congregation lacks sophistication. Sailed right past them. Never saw it coming. Dullards. I grossly overestimated. Creativity killed the preacher. Oh well. No use crying over spilt brilliance. Pearls before swine.

Eighteenth Sunday after Pentecost. Let's see what we've got on deck:

"Hey Pastor, it's the Proper 20! Can't wait to see what you do with that!"

The lectionary? Amos 8:4-7: oppress the poor and needy in Israel. Oh, to beat them over the head with that one! Smack their idiotic seduction by Trump. I've already beaten The Donald to a pulp. Maybe go after Don's sleazy kids? Low-hanging fruit.

First Timothy 2:1-7—God wants "all to be saved and to come to a saving knowledge of God," *apokatastasis*. Love to lay that on them. I've already attacked, but with subtlety, my one incipient Calvinist, stuck a little Wesleyan universalism to 'em. Another punch to the gut is too much.

Luke 16:1-13, the shrewd steward. Guy jilts his boss, then, when discovered, cheats his boss out of the debts others owe him—too lazy for manual labor and too proud to beg—and then is *praised* by the boss he jilted? Let's see what Rick Lischer has to say on this one in his *Reading the Parables*. Check index: "See 'Shrewd,' 'Dishonest.'" Only nine entries? Come on, Rick, give me a handle, my kingdom for a handle on this parable. Lischer's not a biblical scholar anyway! And besides...

Phone rings. "Oh my, so the vestry flower refrigerator died" (budget's behind by 20 percent and we're upset over a refrigerator for flowers!) "No, I have no idea... Can't we just get a secondhand refrigerator... Oh, so that's a stupid idea. That's true, I have no expertise in floral arranging" (thank God). "A 'professional floral refrigerator'? Like the one at the grocery store, for bouquets when you've forgotten your wedding anniversary? You must be kidding... I'm sorry. I know this is serious. Yes, a priority. I assure you that I am committed to quality worship..." *(Jesus!)*

Was that Luke 16 or Luke 15?... Oh well.

Tuesday

Hey, all you bourgeois accommodationists, listen ye to Bev Gaventa: "The parable of the unjust steward has baffled interpreters since the beginning of time." How encouraging. "Jesus's commendation of a dishonest person..." Check out Halvor Moxnes's (real name, *Halvor Moxnes?*) *The Economy of the Kingdom: Social Conflict and Economic Relations in Luke's Gospel* (Minneapolis: Fortress, 1988). Love to drop that on them. "As many of you know, from reading the work of Halvor Moxnes..." "to make friends by unrighteous mammon..." Liberation theology rehash. Come on, Halvor, whatever the story is, it's funny. Maybe I should fall back upon the Epistle? And pass up an opportunity to be with Jesus when he goes weird?

"Shrewd" in 16:8 (*phronimos*) can also be rendered as "prudent" or "wise." Oooh, that's a big help.

Poieiste philous ek tou mamona teis adikias. It's the old *mamona adikias* that gets them every time. I do have a guy who works for Goldman Sachs (Unrighteous Mammon Inc.), so maybe not...

Wednesday

Do or die. Midnight hour. Firing squad. Buckle down. Get rolling. Sunday's our rollout of fall programs, recruitment for Sunday school before it rolls over and dies...

Telephone rings. "Oh, sorry to hear that. Yes, I'm not doing any-thing" (*just preparing to declare the Word of God, that's all!*). "Sure, I'll be right over to the hospital. So glad you called."

Damn.

Thursday

James Joyce, *Dubliners*. Father Purdon and his sermon! Uses this passage. Nice illustration. Some in the congregation fancy themselves as intellectuals. Lay a bit of Joyce upon them.

Telephone rings. "Yes. Mm-hmm…Sorry, they really didn't cover air-conditioning repair in my seminary training.…No, I'm not making light of a serious situation. It's just that I don't know nothing about air conditioning…" *God, give me patience!*

Didn't Tim Keller preach on this text? Surf the web. Yes! "There's no one who is good, no not any. Only God is great." I could have come up with that line all by myself.

"Sometimes you are just way too clever by half." What did Alice Williams mean by that? A compliment? Didn't feel like a compliment when she said it last Sunday before scurrying out of church. Who means "clever" as a compliment?

Mamona adikias. "What the heck is mammon, righteous or un-righteous?" they'll ask. "A part of the feminine anatomy, har, har, har?"

Ah, here's the old reliable C. H. Dodd: "Even Luke is clueless as to what to do with the parable, so he gives three contrasting interpretations at his conclusion." Thanks, Dr. Dodd. So very helpful.

And John Wesley's sermon "The Use of Money"? Let's see what Wesley says of this little hoodlum: "Gain all you can, by common sense, by using in your business all the understanding which God has given you." You think Jesus told this story to laud common sense? Come on, Papa John.

In desperation, back to Lischer! Page 103: "The steward is a liminal figure, neither a child of the night or of the day, but of the twilight, where there is just enough light to get by. We want to have this parable both ways, and we manage it by separating the content of the steward's dubious actions from the resourcefulness with which he carries them out."

Come on, Rick. Bring it back down to earth.

"When our moral strategy is applied to other figures, sports cheaters, murderers, or crooks like Bernie Madoff, the silliness of this approach is quickly unmasked." Silly? Isn't that a bit harsh? Even John Wesley praised the man for "common sense."

Thursday night

Now for the killing spree otherwise known as editing. Choices. The Joyce reference was a great illustration but it will only make 'em feel intellectually inadequate. Though they lie, none of 'em has read James Joyce. Great illustration; dump it. Cheap shot about Trump? Clintons fit just as well. "Who here has not secured yourself with some of this unrighteous mammon?" Spread around the guilt.

"Trump is not the only crook you know!"

"And yet, Jesus makes a sleazy, thieving, lying business guy the hero of his parable?" Nice flip. Lure them in with the anti-Trump; then smack 'em.

It's a metaphor! For God's sake, not a prescription for how to run your business.

Friday

Thought WHAT to say was challenge; GUTS to say what I'm saying, THAT's hard!

"A guy that the Feds would put in the slammer and throw away the key, Jesus makes the hero of this parable."

Nice ending, but what do I do in the meantime?

Saturday

"So sorry, sad..." (*Lady, you think you got problems, take a gander at tomorrow's gospel. I got problems of my own. Saturday afternoon and still empty-handed.*)

Sunday

Oh great, Mary isn't here. She would have lapped up that Joyce illustration. But there's Alice, at least. I'll take Alice if I can't... Who the heck is that couple? Didn't count on there being visitors who don't know how to deal with my sense of humor. They won't know when I'm being ironic! There's George! Better kill the wisecrack about Goldman Sachs Come on. Help me, Jesus!

> "*Um, wasn't that anthem great? That's always been one of my favorites. Since I was a child. Rare that you hear it sung anymore.*

> *Uh, well, let's get going. The gospel for today is, by my reckoning, one of the strangest stories Jesus ever told. I'll just say this: if you are here today hoping for a bit of a moral tune-up, or a few steps to being a better person, a spiritual boost, you Pelagian Methodists, you, well, Jesus got nothing for you.*

> *But, if we'll stick with Jesus, and with the help of a fine commentary on parables by a dear, close friend of mine, well then, maybe Jesus may condescend to speak even to us...*"

The sermon has begun...

Lecture at the retirement of
Richard Lischer, Duke Divinity School,
September 19, 2016

60

Sayings of the Elder

And the LORD spake unto Moses, saying, Take Aaron and his sons with him, and the garments, and the anointing oil, and a bullock for the sin offering, and two rams, and a basket of unleavened bread.... And Moses did as the LORD commanded.... And he ... girded him with the girdle, and clothed him with the robe, and put the ephod upon him, and he girded him with the curious girdle of the ephod, and bound it unto him therewith. And he put the breastplate upon him: also he put in the breastplate the Urim and the Thummim. And he put the mitre upon his head; also upon the mitre, even upon his forefront, did he put the golden plate, the holy crown; as the LORD commanded...

Leviticus 8:1-9 KJV

Thou shalt find thyself a good seminary, one that hath no more than 50 percent of its courses online. Counting a hybrid course as if it were a traditional class is an abomination, no matter what the ATS doth say.

Say unto Aaron and his heirs that I considereth "spiritual formation groups" bogus. If thou wishest to whine about ill-treatment from parents, spouses, or significant others, do it on thine own time! Unbridled narcissism is an abomination unto me.

When thou hast earned thy diploma from an ATS-accredited seminary, present it unto the elders so that they might determine that it is not, in truth, a spurious online degree.

Wear not the holy ephod, breastplates, Urim and Thummim, turban, and curious girdle before thou hast submitted to at least three hours of psychological testing to prove that thou art not a nut, though I care not for thine MMPI profile.

Neither am I greatly troubled by your brush with the law your sophomore year of college. I am full of steadfast mercy, and mine quality is always to forgive. Therefore, the bean-counter regulations of *The*

Book of Discipline or *Book of Church Order* count nothing for the wearing of the *girdle, robe, ephod, the curious girdle, breastplate,* or *the Urim and the Thummim.*

Posting the antics of thine children upon Facebook is an abomination to me. Postings of grandchildren playing soccer are particularly loathsome. Cease! Thou mayest post pictures of your trip to the Holy Land—but only if the congregation has paid for your trip, including incidentals.

Neither thou, nor thy son, nor thy daughter, thy manservant, nor thy maidservant, nor thy cattle, thine ox nor thine ass, nor thy stranger that is within thy gates may use the phrase, "It is what it is."

Thou shalt visit in the homes of thy church members, particularly those who have been negligent in their monthly giving. Guard thy speech when in their living rooms, focusing mostly on sports, the weather, and the doings of the Kardashians.

If thine parishioner is a conservative Republican, thou mayest leave thy calling card in the crack in the front door, ringing the doorbell and sprinting back to thy clerical car and exiting at a high rate of speed. If thou makest thy getaway before they come to the door, thou mayest count that as an annual pastoral visit. Then shalt thou be accredited to wear the *robe, ephod, curious girdle, breastplate,* and *the Urim and the Thummim.*

The most effective pastoral visits are best done between the hours of ten and eleven-fifteen on Monday mornings, when thou hast reasonable certainty that the objects of the visit are otherwise employed.

Believeth not when older women tell thee that their dog's bark is worse than its bite. Feel not the responsibility to visit in a dwelling where there is more than one cat. If thou must visit in a home infested with more than two cats, it is wisdom to wear flea collars on thine ankles, tastefully under the *robe, ephod,* and *the curious girdle.* Thou mayest tell the parishioners that if it were not for thine cat allergy, you wouldest visit. This lie shall not be counted against thee. I grantest unto thee a free pass. For they are a stiff-necked people, adulterous and covetous, whose sins against clergy continue even unto the sixth and seventh generation.

Praise bands, middle-aged accountants twanging on guitars, the beating of bongos, and overly amplified tremulous sopranos I liketh not. Cease!

Thou shalt not download sermons off the web, be they the work of Andy Stanley or even Walter Brueggemann—unless such sermons are stolen for use as a Saturday Night Special on the Sunday after thine annual vacation. I am a merciful One, full of compassion, showing mercy unto the second and third generations of those who fudge on sermon preparation.

Though I maketh the sun to shine on the heads of the righteous and unrighteous, the political pronouncements of Franklin Graham, I liketh not. Cease!

That thou hast been burdened by three funerals—one of them on a Sunday afternoon even though thou hast told the undertaker *NO*, as well as the second wedding of the daughter of thy board chair—none of this is of concern to me and doth not excuse thee from righteous sermon preparation. Cease thy whining and begin exegeting, though thou mayest select a sermon from Willimon's *Pulpit Resource*, if paraphrased. Thou shalt avoid citing Willimon in your sermon since such attribution only inflames those who voted for Trump. Besides, they know not Willimon from Adam. They are a stiff-necked people whose fathers have eaten sour grapes and whose children's teeth are set on edge.

Thou mayest not say, "I'll be praying for you," when thou hast no intention of doing so, and are not even sure of the name of the person with whom thou talkest. However, thou mayest say, without fear of my reprisal, "Lots of luck."

Thou mayest not say, when offered a higher-paying pastorate, that thou and thine spouse are "praying for wise discernment" when in truth thou art already packing and negotiating for a higher travel allowance with the new church.

Thou shalt not roll thine eyes when confronted by the inane comments of the chair of your church board; neither shalt thou refer to thy trustee chair as, "Idiot," though thou mayest do so in the privacy of thy parsonage with thine lawfully wedded spouse.

In thine Stewardship Sunday sermons, thou needest not trouble thyself about scripture, theology, or even clear thinking. Thou art off the hook. Keep thine eyes on the bottom line. They are a stiff-necked people who loathe to part with their cash. Get the job done, put the squeeze on them, and show to me that thou art worthy to wear the *robe, ephod, the curious girdle, breastplate,* and *the Urim and the Thummim.*

Thou shalt not covet thy neighboring pastor's ox or ass, spouse, executive wash room, parsonage, even if his parsonage hath a pool. Thou shalt not covet thy neighboring pastor's travel allowance, two-month vacation, nor anything that is thy neighbor's. Yet thou mayest use that neighbor's salary when trying to shame thy board during yearly salary negotiations. Then shalt thou wear the *coat, robe, ephod, the curious girdle, breastplate,* and *the Urim and the Thummim.*

When thou receivest a plaster set of praying hands, spray painted gold, for the coffee table in the parsonage, thou shouldest thank the giver of the gift as if thou wast, in truth, pleased, though thou mayest stash the praying hands in a closet until the annual Christmas drop-in without fear of wrath. Lying is one thing; stupidity is unforgivable.

Good luck as thou goest thy priestly way in life. Never trust the music director, nor paid soloists. Go thy way, acting humble, adorned in *robe, ephod, the curious girdle, breastplate,* and *the Urim and the Thummim.*

Suggested by Ian Frazier's
"Lamentations of the Father,"
Selected Shorts, 2018

61

Happy Lent

Her failure was irrefutable. The project had ended in disaster. She thought back on all the meetings where she had argued for the initiative, the skill with which she answered every objection. This was "her baby," her great, innovative, surefire idea that couldn't fail.

But the numbers were dismal and undeniable. This big, career-ending fiasco was hers and hers alone to bear. This dud had her name all over it.

Of course, this would be the end of her time with the company. Where, in God's name, would she get a job after this public flop?

So, she agonizingly decided to walk in, take the rap, and resign. That way maybe the boss would cool down and write her a recommendation good enough to get another job elsewhere.

First thing the next morning, after a sleepless, tearful night, she walked in and told her supervisor, "Goodbye. I'm going in first thing today and admit to the boss what's happened. Take full responsibility. Hope he doesn't kill me as he fires me. Bad way for me to end with the company. No one else to blame."

"I've fixed it," said her supervisor. "Went in yesterday afternoon and told the boss that we thought the project was a great idea and that you did all our homework. We were all on board, but it wasn't to be. Told him about the losses and said it was all my fault."

"*You did what?* But it was my problem! You only signed off on it because I told you it couldn't fail. What did the boss say?" she asked.

"Oh, he blew his stack, as expected. Ranted and raved. Told me that he was disappointed in my leadership. Told me that I had better not mess up again, and a bunch of other stuff."

"You took the blame for my mistake? You did that for me?" she said, dumbfounded by what her supervisor had done. "Nobody does that."

The supervisor smiled and said, "*He* did. Happy Lent."

62
My Dog, the Methodist

At the United Methodist Church's 1988 General Conference, we voted to make 9 million new United Methodists by 1992. Southern Baptists scoffed; how could a denomination that has managed to lose 65,000 members every year somehow come up with many millions of Methodists in the next few years? Last year we couldn't even find more than 200,000 new Methodists. So, where do we expect to find the other 9 million?

In four years at my previous parish—despite my earnest efforts to apply the principles of the Church Growth Movement—I found only about 150 new United Methodists, and some of them weren't any better at being Methodist than they were being Baptist or Presbyterian or whatever they were before I found them. So, I had about decided that our goal of 9 million new members would make us the laughingstock of everybody in COCU (Conference on Christian Unity).

Then, in the course of my scholarly duties, I came upon a brilliant but neglected monograph by Charles M. Nielsen of Colgate-Rochester Divinity School, titled *Communion for Dogs* (German title, *Abendmahl Für Hunde*, Perspectives in Religious Studies, Mercer University). Building upon the groundbreaking work of Peter Singer's *Animal Liberation* (Avon, 1977) and basing his thesis on all sorts of footnotes—biblical, patristic, medieval, and Reformation—Dr. Nielsen makes a convincing argument that dogs should be admitted to the Lord's Table in Reformed churches:

> Reformed churches used to stress discipline, but now it is clear that we train our dogs far better than we train our children. Since…dogs [are not] self-centered, egocentric or selfish, they are now the only appropriate Christ symbols. They are loyal, adorable, loving, and caring and clearly should be allowed to receive communion.

It is fair to say that *Communion for Dogs* gives all dogs a new leash on life, so to speak.

Being a Methodist, my concern is not who should come to the Lord's Supper (which we don't celebrate that often, anyway) but where in the world we expect to find a million new members. But after reading Nielsen, I knew: right in my own home, sleeping even now in my garage, is a willing convert—Polly, a black terrier of uncertain parentage and quixotic disposition.

All over this fair nation, there are many millions of Polly's compatriots who have been neglected, ignored, and even scorned by evangelistic efforts. Yet they already possess all of the characteristics for membership in one of today's most progressive denominations: openness, spontaneity, affirmation, inclusiveness, love, righteous indignation, sexual freedom, gut reactions.

Here are our 9 million new Methodists! Why has the Christian church heretofore overlooked dogs as fit recipients of the good news? The answer is simple: bigotry, close-mindedness, and prejudice. No doubt many of you immediately call to mind Revelation 22:15, which lists those who are refused admission into the eternal bliss of heaven: "Outside are the dogs and sorcerers and fornicators and murderers and idolaters" (NRSV). But what does that proof text prove?

I've served churches where murderers may have been scarce, but fornicators were not. Besides, we have learned to jettison so much of scripture with which we don't agree, so why should we preserve the obviously anti-canine sentiments of Revelation 22:15?

All scripture must be read by dog lovers with a "hermeneutic of suspicion"; the Bible simply gives dogs a bad rap. Even though Genesis 9 asserts that covenant is established "with every living being with you—with the birds, with the large animals, and with all the animals of the earth, leaving the ark" (v. 10), traditional exegesis has acted as if every beast and creature were on the ark except for Polly's ancestors. If her ancestors hated water as much as Polly does when I try to give her a bath, I can assure you that no ark would have left port without dogs on board.

You will no doubt say that this anti-canine prejudice merely reflects the culture-bound nature of Scripture and that we have at last overcome this bias. Don't be so sure! When Billy Graham preached at our chapel, I asked him how many dogs he had converted. This man—who had gone to the ends of the earth to preach—looked at me as if I were crazy. I guess that I shouldn't have expected better of someone who admired the likes of Charles G. Finney, who wrote in his *Lectures on Revivals of Religion*:

> People should leave their dogs, and very young children at home. I have often known contentions arise among dogs...just at that stage of the services, that would most effectually destroy the effect of the meeting....As for dogs, they had infinitely better be dead, than to divert attention from the word of God. See that deacon; perhaps his dog has in this way destroyed more souls than the deacon will ever be instrumental in saving.

Even the so-called *Inclusive Language Lectionary*—while making such a fuss over the sexism and patriarchal nature of Scripture and going to such extreme efforts to delete it from the hearing of modern, more enlightened Christian congregations—totally ignores the Bible's anti-canine bias. The *Inclusive Language Lectionary* prides itself on its reworking of such passages as Hebrews 11 to read: "By faith Abraham [and Sarah] obeyed when they were called to go out to a place...and they went out, not knowing where they were to go." But what about Abraham and Sarah's dogs? Did the dogs who faithfully followed them into an unknown land know the route any better than Abraham and Sarah? Did their following require any less faith? No! In fact, the dogs had to have more faith than Abraham and Sarah since they were following human beings who admittedly had no idea of where they were going.

Of course, there will always be those who object to such hermeneutics because the original text doesn't say that Abraham (or Sarah) had a dog. But their very objection proves my point. In telling the story, most backward, conservative, biased, bourgeois people have completely and intentionally overlooked the contributions of dogs. Do you find dogs mentioned in the stories of Jacob, Joseph, Moses, David, Bathsheba, Esther, or Ruth? I rest my case.

For the intractably reactionary, other texts must also be considered. For instance, is not my thesis that Polly is a potential United Methodist vitiated by Matthew 7:6: "Don't give dogs holy things; and don't throw your pearls in front of pigs"? Careful exegesis shows that this text cannot be taken seriously. *Kusin* is an ancient metaphor for wicked people. The dogs here being disparaged are simply not dogs.

Then there is that unfortunate slip by Paul in Philippians 3:2: "Look out for the dogs." Dr. Nielsen notes that the "dogs" here were possibly Jewish Christians. Therefore, rather than being a term of opprobrium, "Watch out for the 'dogs'" is an early reference to fellow Christians. "You old dog, you," when spoken by one Christian to another, is a term of endearment.

Besides, even if these texts do say nasty things about canines, we have been so successful at removing Jesus's strictures against divorce, riches, violence, and adultery, so why can't we dispose of Matthew 7:6 and Philippians 3:2 as well?

I believe there is clear biblical warrant for dogs as fit subjects for baptism—even though Polly hates baths. In defending infant baptism, scholars such as Oscar Cullmann and Joachim Jeremias give weight to what is called the "*oikos* formula" (from the Greek word for "household"), noting that, at a number of places in Acts, someone is baptized "and his whole household with him." Even though children are not explicitly mentioned, these great scholars assume that children were also members of the household and were therefore baptized at an early age.

Well, how many dog owners do you know who do not consider their pet to be a part of the household? We always take ours with us when we go to the beach, to the park, to the grandparents' house. Isn't it reasonable, then, to assume that the primitive church would have taken these beloved household pets along for baptism?

We talk to dogs, kiss them, cuddle them, and toilet train them (more rapidly than we can train our children). So, if children can be baptized, so can dogs. What is more, we have now progressed to the point where our dogs eat and dress like us, have beauty parlors, cemeteries, psychologists, and birth control devices—and we have become like them in our sexual behavior. So, I see no biblical objection to any congregation receiving them as full communicants.

Schleiermacher defined religion as "a feeling of absolute dependence" rather than "an instinctive craving for a mess of metaphysical and ethical crumbs"? Methodists are not too big on theological speculation. Similarly, I have never seen Polly bothered by metaphysics or ethics. (She may indulge in such in the privacy of our garage, but I doubt it.)

Polly knows that she is absolutely dependent on my keeping the urologist next door from killing her when he went out unannounced to retrieve his morning paper. Polly is as religious as the average Methodist. G. W. F. Hegel countered Schleiermacher by saying that, if religion were merely a feeling of absolute dependence, then "a dog would be the best Christian."

If we United Methodists give Polly the right hand of fellowship and a pledge card, we'll be well on our way toward that goal of 9 million new members. On second thought, let's forget the right hand of fellowship and just tell her how glad we are to have her in church. Polly may have the heart of a Methodist, but she still has the teeth of a pagan.

I rest my case.

The Christian Century, July 16, 1989

63

Polly's Passing

In case you haven't heard, our dog Polly died recently. Until 1989 Polly was little known outside our family—except among meter readers and delivery persons. (Of Polly no one ever said, "Her bark is worse than her bite.") Then, in the article "My Dog, the Methodist," Polly made her theological debut. Concerned that the United Methodist General Conference didn't have a prayer of reaching its goal of adding 9 million new Methodists to its rolls in four years, I proposed that we declare dogs fit subjects for baptism. My argument was buttressed by theological rationale. Through exacting biblical analysis, I demonstrated Polly's readiness for baptism.

Readers were unimpressed. Two United Methodist bishops refused to speak to me, and the *Christian Century* lost three subscribers. "Will someone at Duke please find something for Willimon to do?" asked one reader. The evangelization of dogs has not been mentioned again in that magazine. Polly remained unbaptized; United Methodist losses continued unabated.

As for Polly's personal theological views, she was unimpressed by recent developments in womanist theology, showed no interest in the work of John Cobb, exhibited no need to be informed about church growth strategies, and treated visiting Jehovah's Witnesses, Mormons, and even neighborhood-canvassing Baptists with the same opprobrium and contempt she showed the UPS. She resisted all attempts to bring news to our home by the *Durham Morning Herald*.

Having been rejected for baptism, she hated both the message and the messenger.

A pastoral counselor colleague explained that Polly's behavior was typical of the Rejected-for-Baptism Syndrome (RFBS). The rejected one reacts with vicious counter rejection. My friend has observed this behavior only among Baptists, never among Methodists.

"I've never heard of Methodists refusing to do anything anyone asked of them," he said, in love.

Although she spurned the organized religion that had precluded her, throughout her fifteen years of life, Polly remained a loyal member of our family. Having helped raise our two children from infancy, her attitude in her declining years appeared to be, "I endured the both of them, correcting many of your parental mistakes and following you people through a succession of inadequate yards and cold carports. Now, you owe me."

Two years ago, when I took Polly to the veterinarian for a routine inoculation, I was presented with a bill for $160.50 and told, "This is Polly's geriatric exam." Yes, Polly had reached the ripe old age of fourteen, no small feat for a dog that had survived flying thirty feet through the air after being hit by a car; having her head grazed by the rear tire of our neighbor's station wagon; and living with our two children. The veterinarian advised a regimen of estrogen pills, membership in the American Association of Retired Persons, and ceramics classes at the Baptist church, along with trips to see the leaves change in the mountains with the Episcopalians.

Polly mangled my hand when I attempted to force upon her the estrogen, just as she had always responded to attempts to medicate her. Being opposed to all mail, she would have nothing to do with the AARP. Having been rejected by the Methodists, she refused risking a repeat experience with the Baptists, or even the more ingratiating Anglicans. Without benefit of clergy, she lived almost two more years.

On her last day, of life, she roused herself briefly in the morning, staggered out of the garage, and collapsed. She gazed at our mailbox, recalling earlier days of protest against representatives of the US government. Wistfully she looked toward our neighbor's yard and remembered how she had rid it of an impertinent cat one warm day in May. I carried her back to the garage and placed her in her bed. She groaned, not from pain, I think, but at the final indignity of falling so dependently into inept human hands. "You shall be as I, one day," were her last words to me. "You may be a human, even a baptized one—big deal. But you and I are closer kin than you like to admit."

That afternoon, returning from purchasing a Christmas tree, I petted her on the head. She looked up at me with infinite weariness, not so much sad to be leaving this world as peeved to be exiting before me. She sighed and was gone. Some believe she died of a tired heart, weakened by fifteen years of reckless pursuit of all kinds and conditions of vehicles. I, however, felt she simply could not endure another Christian festival from which she, solely by circumstance of birth, was excluded.

The Christian Century, April 20, 1994

64
Where Did Jesus Say . . . ?

At our men's prayer and Bible study breakfast (God and a sausage biscuit at an ungodly hour) the topic for the morning was gun control in America. We predictably split into two groups. Half said that guns are essential for self-defense. The only response to a bad guy with a gun is a good guy with a bigger gun. That's the problem, said the other half. Too many guns. Our plethora of guns give no adequate self-defense but actually make safely defending ourselves more difficult.

"While we may disagree about gun control, it's nice to see that we all agree on one basic principle: self-defense," I said, finding common ground. "We may quibble about how best to defend ourselves, but we all agree that self-defense is a common good."

Then one of the men (an accountant!) asked, "Preacher, I can't recall one instance of anybody practicing self-defense in the New Testament. Can you?"

"I'll get back with you," said I. This man an accountant!

How Odd of God: Chosen for the Curious Vocation of Preaching, Westminster John Knox Press, 2015

65
Called to Write

I got the call to write before I was called to preach. The week before our grand trek from Greenville to Colorado Springs for the 1960 National Jamboree, Scouts of the Blue Ridge Council received last-minute instruction. Scout executives announced the lackeys whom they had tapped for senior patrol leader, chaplain, patrol leaders, and quartermaster. "Williamson? Williston? Willerman? You are troop scribe." *Scribe? What's that?* "You write reports to the chief scout executive. He'll send them to the *Greenville News* if they're newsworthy."

What's "newsworthy"?

As our overburdened, dilapidated buses belched through Kentucky, I got the guts to ask the scoutmaster why I had been selected as scribe. "The popular boys were chosen as troop leaders," he explained. "You gotta take what's left."

Every couple of days I dutifully mailed my dispatches to Mr. Stanley. Knowing that old man Stanley hired the ancient buses that broke down in Oklahoma, I described eighty boys sweltering on the side of the road awaiting a mechanic. Thank God for the first aid merit badge, I wrote, or we could have died in Soonerland. I quoted comments about Stanley's logistical mismanagement. I informed my readers of the wasteland between Louisville and Colorado Springs; don't bother taking the trip. I testified to the rundown motel in Missouri where we were delighted by the pool but unhappy about being awakened throughout the night by men banging on our doors, calling out, "Myrtle? Are you in there? I paid! Myrtle? It's my time." I disclosed how Henry Taylor—who had climbed on the roof to retrieve his hatchet that had been thrown out the window during an argument—was locked out and forced to shiver in his briefs on the roof of Bates Motel until dawn.

Once at the Jamboree, I described the stew made by Scouts from the Congo—a week's rations dumped in one smoldering pot from which they ladled three brownish meals a day, reasoning, "It all goes to the same stomach." I marveled that Scouts from Texas conned New Yorkers out of fully embroidered Order of the Arrow patches, swapping them for horned toads that they swore made you hallucinate if you licked them.

I exposed the Scouts from Georgia who traded cockleburs nestled in small boxes of cotton to unsuspecting dolts from New Jersey as "Genuine Porcupine Eggs. Keep at 71 degrees for two weeks." I noted that President Eisenhower looked too old to be running the country, and that the Scouts from Laurens were vowing never to get back on the Buses of Death even if they had to break up with their girlfriends and stay in Colorado through high school.

When we finally limped back home (including the Scouts from Laurens, who were forced on the bus by a scoutmaster screaming, "I don't give a rip who your old man is!"), a crowd welcomed us at the Trailways bus depot. A reporter among them shouted, "Which one of you is—pardon my alliteration—*William Willimon*?" He waved a wad of clippings from the *Greenville News* with headlines "Scouts' Travail in Tennessee" and "Scouts Unimpressed by Presidential Visit."

"Hey, Walter Winchell Willimon. Your column got moved from the last page to the front after your second posting! How 'bout a big smile for your readers? The newsroom heard them Northerners are still sittin' on them porcupine eggs. What'd you Scouts think of that whorehouse in Missouri?"

My mother said little on the way home except, "Next time you engage in journalism, remember that, unlike you, I'm staying in Greenville."

Accidental Preacher: A Memoir, William
B. Eerdmans Publishing Company, 2019

66
How I Got My Job

On a recent Sunday, after an especially subtle sermon, some nice person had deposited a note in the offering plate. The student usher delivered the note to me with particular glee: "Listening to your sermon today, I had to ask myself how a fool like you had been hired by Duke University."

Here's how.

I was minding my business at a small church in Greenville, South Carolina, when the telephone rang. I picked it up and was surprised to hear a familiarly accented voice saying,

"Dr. Willimon, this is Terry Sanford up at Duke. I am surprised that you don't have a secretary."

"Er, uh, my secretary left early today."

"How small is your church?" he asked.

Then he explained to me that he was looking for a preacher at Duke and some people had told him that he ought to be looking at me. After a bit more conversation, he invited me to come up to Duke, take a look at the job, and meet with him.

"What makes you think that I might be your person?" I asked.

"I don't know that you are. I have never heard of you. People tell me you are real good as a preacher. I also like the fact that you answer your own telephone."

How could I refuse such an overture? The next week, I was visiting on the Duke campus. I arrived at the president's guest house late one spring afternoon. In about an hour, there was a knock at the door of my room and there was President Sanford. We sat down by the fireplace in the guest house.

"I have a great job here for a preacher, for the right kind of preacher. Duke Chapel is one of the most beautiful churches in the world, if I picked you. Do you know the governor of South Carolina?"

After an "Er, uh," I began to talk about my theological orientation, the sorts of ministerial activities I enjoy, my vision for the future of the church.

"How small is your church?" Mr. Sanford asked.

"Oh, we have about four hundred members—but we are growing," I replied defensively.

"I bet we have about that many in our choir alone at Duke Chapel," said Mr. Sanford.

I continued to talk about my theology of Christian ministry. In the middle of my exposition, Mr. Sanford asked, "Do you know any Democrats in South Carolina?"

"I know a lot of Democrats. Like, my grandmother," I said.

I told him that I also knew personally the coroner of Greenville County. This seemed to please him.

Rambling on about ministry for another couple of minutes, I was interrupted by Mr. Sanford saying, "I'll be back in touch."

About two weeks later, I received a call from President Sanford at home, inviting me to come to Duke.

"It looks like you are the preacher I've been looking for," he said.

I returned to Duke for more visits with staff and students, house hunting, and other matters. Periodically, I inquired when I might be meeting with President Sanford again. One detail he had never mentioned was salary. Thus, it was with great anticipation that I awaited him on Wednesday morning for our appointment. He appeared about 9 a.m. and invited me into his office

"Now, let's see...we need to talk about details of the job. Just what is it we need to discuss?"

I began by saying that I really thought I was interested in the job, but I realized we had never talked about salary. I told him that while salary was not my main consideration, it was an important factor.

"Have you ever tried to get a broken glass out of a disposal in a sink?" Mr. Sanford interrupted.

"What?"

"Yeah, you know, like a small juice glass. This morning I dropped a glass down our disposal and Margaret Rose told me not to leave the house until I got it out. Now, how would you get out that glass?" asked Mr. Sanford.

"Well, I guess, I might try to take a dish cloth and stick it down the disposal and pull the glass out with that," I said.

"Are you crazy?" he asked. "You want me to cut my hand? Think of something else."

"Well then, I might try a pair of tongs," I offered.

"A pair of tongs?" he asked, laughing heartily. "Well, what were you saying about details?"

I made an effort to continue my discussion about the job. After about four minutes of my talking, Mr. Sanford suddenly wheeled around in his chair, picked up the telephone receiver, dialed, and said, "Joe. I need some help. How would you get a broken glass out of a disposal? I've got a preacher here who says he might try to lift it out with a pair of tongs."

He listened on the telephone.

"Yeah, I know. That's what I told him. Preachers aren't plumbers!" he laughed jovially. "Well, any help you can give me would be appreciated. Margaret Rose is going to give me hell if I don't get that glass out of there by noon. Thanks." He put down the receiver and wheeled around in his chair, again facing me.

"Well, what was that you were saying?" he asked.

For the life of me, I had no idea. All I could do was think about other possible means of retrieving a glass from a disposal.

"I think I was saying something about salary."

"Salary, money, money," said Mr. Sanford. "For a preacher, you sure are interested in money. Of course, lots of preachers I have known are mighty interested in money. Is there nothing else you wanted to talk about?"

I confessed that I had nothing else in mind to discuss. With that, Mr. Sanford stood up, grasped my hand warmly, shook it, and told me how glad he was to have me "on board here at Duke." He promised me that we would have another visit in a few weeks when we could discuss the details. "Tell Governor Riley hello for me when you see him," he said.

As I attempted to respond, he wheeled around and grabbed his coat, saying, "Well, this has all been great. But I've got to go to New York City right now. I'm gonna have some people by to talk to you, let you meet a bunch of people tomorrow, get a feel for the place. I'll be back in touch."

"I do have one request. Please let me announce this to my church. They have no clue that they might be losing their pastor. Please don't announce this until after next Sunday," I said.

That Friday Mr. Sanford told the Duke trustees, "I've hired us a good preacher." My people heard it on the radio thirty minutes after he announced it to the board.

When, three weeks later, I returned to Durham, I still had no official letter hiring me at Duke and absolutely no salary figure. I was told that Mr. Sanford wished to meet with me at his home.

I eagerly arrived at the President's House, determined not to leave until I had a very clear picture in my mind about my new job. Mr. Sanford met me at the door and invited me in. We chatted briefly, and then he said, "Now, as I remember, we had some details you wanted to talk about. I've got a letter I have composed that I plan to send to you. I'd like to read it to you and see what you think."

I was delighted at last to be getting down to business. Mr. Sanford began to read, "'Dear Dr. Willimon...'"

"That is an earned doctorate?" he asked.

"Yes, it is," I said. "Is that important to the job?"

"Of course not," said Mr. Sanford. "But around this place, a lot of people judge people on the basis of their titles. I just wanted to be sure before I went on."

After he had read a couple of opening sentences, he paused, looked at me and said, "How do you cook country ham in South Carolina?"

"Country ham? Er, uh, I guess we would probably bake it and—"

"No! That's what Margaret Rose always says. She's from Kentucky and thinks she knows everything about ham. I have been given some great country ham. I want to fry it. She doesn't like it that way. If she shows up here and asks you, don't you tell her that you would bake ham. Tell her that you would fry it," he ordered.

I assured Mr. Sanford that I would tell her anything he wanted, as long as he kept reading the letter. He continued. He read a couple of more gracious but vague sentences and then he said, "I'm hot. Thirsty. You want some lemonade?"

I told him that I would be glad to have lemonade, barely concealing my annoyance. With that, he took the letter with him in the kitchen and began to make lemonade. The only reason I agreed to lemonade was that I thought he already had lemonade.

"How much sugar do you like in your lemonade?" he called from the kitchen.

I told him to use however much sugar he liked, muttering under my breath that I didn't give a rip whether it had sugar or not, just so he got back in here and resumed reading the letter. The thing had gotten on my mind now and I was becoming obsessed.

After either fifteen minutes or two hours, he emerged, proudly bearing two large glasses of lemonade. He sat down, giving me my glass of lemonade, and, after taking a self-satisfied sip of his, he started over, beginning to read the letter. He got no further than the first three sentences he had previously read when he stopped and commented, "It's hot in here. Let's go out and sit on my porch. I have the nicest porch."

I glumly followed.

On his porch, we settled into two rocking chairs, and Mr. Sanford resumed reading. Out in the front yard below us, a workman was cutting down an old tree with a chainsaw. When Mr. Sanford finally began mumblingly reading the letter, the workman started his chain saw. Mr. Sanford was reading, in a low, gravelly sort of voice. Like the way you do when somebody tells you a dirty joke, I slid my rocking chair over closer to him. I heard no more than every other word. In the middle of his reading, he looked up at me and slid his chair away about four inches, uneasily.

"I'm sorry, I can't hear you," I said in a shout.

He stood up and, with some aggravation, called, "Joe! Joe! Cut off that chainsaw. I am trying to read a letter to this preacher. Yeah, cut off the chainsaw. The saw!"

Whoever Joe was, he turned off the chain saw. "I've got a preacher up here who is real concerned about how much money he is going to get if he comes to work at Duke."

Joe called back up to us that he was a Baptist and had a preacher just like that.

Mr. Sanford resumed reading. By that time, I was so disoriented I could not remember why I was there. I could not for sure remember who I was, or the purpose of the letter in the first place. By the time Mr. Sanford finished, looked up to me, and asked, "Well, does that about get it?"

I said, "Yes. I'll take it."

Mr. Sanford showed me to the door, patted me on the back, shook my hand, and told me how much I was going to enjoy working at Duke. I do remember asking, "About how many times a year do you think I should preach in the chapel?"

"Oh, we can work that out when you get here."

"But I wondered if you could give me an idea of your general expectations for how many sermons I would be preaching in the chapel," I persisted.

"How should I know that now?" he asked. "Why, I haven't even heard you preach yet. Let me hear you preach a few times, and then I can come up with a firm number."

With that, I left. A month later, I and my family moved to Durham.

To this day, I cannot recall where I put that letter Mr. Sanford read to me that spring afternoon on his porch. I remember only one phrase, something about, "Nevertheless, I am offering you the best job you ever had, among some of the best people you'll ever meet, at the most beautiful church ever built."

Mr. Sanford was right.

Duke Dialogue, January 22, 1993

67

Preacher's Coming

My cousin Jim Gibson—you may know him: a lawyer in Beaufort—says that when he was a boy, he and his daddy were working out in the field one hot, low-country afternoon. They looked up and saw his older sister running out to the field, shouting, "Daddy, the preacher's here, and Mama says to come in and help her keep him company."

Jim's daddy hardly looked up, saying to Jim's sister, "Preacher? What kind of preacher?"

"She didn't say."

"Son," his daddy said, "go on back to the house with your sister. If it's the Methodist preacher, latch the door to the smokehouse. If it's the Episcopal preacher, you be sure my liquor cabinet is locked. If it's the Baptist preacher, you go sit in Mama's lap 'till I get there."

68

The Evangelization of a Family Named Fulp

A Parable, with Apologies to E. B. White and the Church Growth Movement

In a sparsely populated corner of southern Iowa, there lived a farm family by the name of Fulp. There were six Fulps. They farmed a hundred-acre plot of corn wedged between broad expanses of wheat fields, with an occasional house. The Fulps subsisted on what they grew in their garden, plus canned salmon, three turkeys a year, shredded wheat, and one carton of soft drinks per week.

The Fulps were contented folk who minded their own business and gave rides to hitchhikers (if they passed any) when they drove their pickup truck into town (seven miles away) for groceries each Saturday afternoon. They usually voted a straight Republican ticket. On the

Fourth of July, they set off a few firecrackers. In winter they mostly sat by the fire and watched reruns of *Gilligan's Island* and had popcorn and hot chocolate. On Saturday evenings, after all the little Fulps were in bed, Mr. and Mrs. Fulp each had a glass of Mogen David before retiring. On Sundays they slept late, occasionally arising in time to watch Oral Roberts.

No Fulp had ever been a member of anything—except for Mr. Fulp's brief stint in the American Legion after the war. The Fulps were not opposed to clubs or organized activities; the fact of the matter was that they had never been moved to seek membership. When a Fulp felt the need of companionship or intellectual stimulation, he or she simply sat down with another Fulp or else forgot about it.

One October, the Methodist, Baptist, and Presbyterian churches in town got worked up over evangelism and launched a big community crusade to attract the unchurched. The Lutherans were worked up too, but since they were between pastors, they did not participate. The churches rented a billboard on the road into town and posted a message for the unchurched with a phone number for them to call if they were interested. The churches also took out a full-page ad in the weekly newspaper, listing the hours when they had worship services. Prayer and study groups met each week in members' homes in town, to study why the unchurched were that way and to pray that they would change. They studied a book by a religion professor at Wilson College, available for $3.50 from Artos Publishers, Inc.

The Methodists and Baptists met each night for a week, sang some songs, prayed, took up a collection, and heard an evangelist from Texas who told them that their churches would "dry up and die" and be "as bad off as the Episcopalians" if they did not get some new members and if there was not a "rebirth of commitment to Christ." The Methodists hired an expert from Nashville who came in for a day and told them about the Church Growth Movement and said that what they needed to do was reach out and love and go to where the people were. The

Methodists decided to start a bridge club in their fellowship hall for the town's senior citizens.

As for the Baptists, they hired a man from Nashville who came in for a day and told them that what they needed was to do a community religious survey to determine where the unchurched were, to ask them why they were unchurched, and to get them churched. The Baptists did the survey, knocking on every door within a ten-mile radius. The survey revealed that the pickings were slim, so far as the unchurched were concerned. One lapsed Roman Catholic, an angry Baptist who was still mad about having lost out in the row over the church parking lot, and a woman who said that she went out of town to visit her aunt every weekend—these were the sole prospects to be found.

Except for a family outside of town by the name of Fulp.

When two women from the Baptist church, accompanied by a woman from the Presbyterian church, called on the Fulps, they were welcomed warmly by Mrs. Fulp, who offered them coffee, and by the little Fulps, who, in responding to the women's questions, informed them that they were five, eight, ten, and fourteen respectively and that Mr. Fulp was fixing the gears on the tractor. After a while, Mr. Fulp came in and the women talked to him too.

The women, upon discovering that the Fulps were utterly un-churched, encouraged them to decide on one of the town's churches and to start attending. They also urged the little Fulps to come to Sunday school, where they would be with lots of other nice boys and girls. The Presbyterian admitted that her church had too few children to have a Sunday school but added that they did have a nice young minister fresh out of seminary. One of the leaders from the Baptist church told Mrs. Fulp that the Baptists taught only the Bible in their Sunday school and that their church youth group went on a choir tour to New Orleans every spring.

The Fulps listened politely, asked no questions, thanked the women for coming, and told them to come back anytime they wished. Mr. Fulp excused himself and went back out to work on the tractor.

After rushing back into town, the women alerted their pastors to the plight of the Fulps. One said she detected that the Fulps seemed to be searching for something. Another visitor noted that Mrs. Fulp had a pleasant voice and could probably sing in a church choir. The pastors speculated that Mr. Fulp was probably your irresponsible type of father but that he could possibly be reached if he were visited by a couple of businessmen from town.

The response of the churches and their members was immediate and gratifying. A prayer group covenanted to pray for the Fulps each day, at noon and at four-thirty. The owner of the Ford dealership in town volunteered to visit Mr. Fulp, while a delegation of women called on Mrs. Fulp on six separate occasions, taking her a chocolate pie and a cassette recording of an inspirational address by Dale Evans. Members of the youth group at the Baptist church decided to adopt the Fulps as their fall project and to have a party for the two older Fulp children. The Methodists focused on the two younger Fulps, mailing them a "We Missed You" postcard each Sunday after Sunday school. Local merchants were asked to watch for the Fulps when they came into town on Saturday afternoons and to try to get a commitment from them to attend church the next day. All of the ministers called upon the Fulps every week, each one leaving a stack of membership materials from his church and a copy of the *Upper Room*. The Methodist minister spent an afternoon explaining, in some detail, the Methodist Social Principles and clarifying why the church's General Board of Discipleship had gone on record recently in favor of binding arbitration in labor disputes.

The Fulps themselves were a bit overwhelmed by all the attention. The little Fulps started attending church youth groups, which meant that they were hardly ever home anymore. Mrs. Fulp now spent most of her day on the telephone, talking to women from the various churches, or else listening to her latest cassette of *The Total Woman*. Mr. Fulp stopped making the weekly pilgrimage into town on Saturday with his family since he felt harassed in every store where they shopped. He also started avoiding Mrs. Fulp after she returned from town one Saturday with a pair of hot-pink baby doll pajamas. Eventually, Mr. and Mrs. Fulp stopped speaking to each other altogether after a three-hour argument one night over prevenient grace. The fourteen-year-old Fulp, who had learned to smoke on a recent youth retreat, was becoming insufferably rebellious.

Finally, the pressure got to Mr. Fulp. One night, after their new practice of family devotionals, he climbed into his pickup truck and headed for Des Moines, never to be heard from again. It is assumed that he probably perished there as a wino, following several months of dissipation. The younger Fulps became regular Sunday school attenders, two at the Baptist church and one at the Methodist church. The eldest Fulp offspring ran away with a seventeen-year-old majorette while they were in New Orleans together on the spring choir tour. From New Orleans they made their way to California, where it is rumored that they now live together out of wedlock.

Mrs. Fulp sold the farm and moved into town, where she was led to join the Presbyterian church, an action on her part that led nearly half of the women in town to vow never to speak to her again and that led the Methodist minister to phone the Presbyterian minister and tell him what he thought of his proselyting. The Baptist minister said that he had detected, early in his acquaintance with Mrs. Fulp, that she was emotionally unstable, and he hoped that the Presbyterians could give her whatever it was that she was looking for.

Mrs. Fulp now does workshops in parent effectiveness training and can be booked through the Presbyterian synod office at 203 Maguire Street, Iowa City, Iowa 52240.

The Christian Century,
September 13, 1978

69
The Visit

I knocked at the door of the little house. It was my second week in this parish, my second week of working my way through the homes of my new congregation. I had dressed casually to help people feel at ease. Sarah Jones was visit number eighteen. "Mrs. Jones?" I asked the small figure that peered at me through the shaded screen door.

"You're here at last!" she said in a jovial tone. "I've been hoping you might come by this week. I'm thrilled to see you."

Although I was surprised that she'd been waiting for me—I considered my door-to-door visitation to be supererogation—I was pleased that she was glad I'd come. After I sat down on her rose-colored couch, she asked, "Now that you're at last here" (*At last? Come on, lady, I've been in town for only two weeks!*) "what do you need from me?"

"Need? Well, nothing really. I first wanted to get to know you better," I said. She seemed annoyed. Perhaps she was the shy type. I would have to draw her out.

"Let's begin by you telling me something about your family," I said. "How long have you been a widow?"

"Ten years," she said wistfully. "Paul died ten years ago last month."

"I'm sorry. How did he die?"

"Well," she said with some obvious discomfort, "he took his own life."

"I'm sorry," I said again. "And your children?"

"I have two," she said. And two grandchildren. I heard about Paul Jr.'s job in Seattle, about Sarah Lea's work as an attorney. I was all ears. When told about Sarah Lea's divorce, I prodded her to describe how she felt about that. We explored her ambivalence toward her son-in-law, his infidelities and sexual indiscretions. When told that Sarah Lea's marriage was "doomed from the beginning," I asked what she meant by that. As it turns out, Sarah Lea became pregnant her junior year of college and felt forced into the marriage, even though she secretly despised the groom.

From here our conversation turned back to Sarah's own marriage. I asked her about her negative feelings about her husband's death. When she said she "couldn't help feeling guilty," I asked her to elaborate. She was reluctant, but with some additional pastoral encouragement she discussed her feelings, occasionally wiping tears from her eyes.

"But why must we talk about such things?" Sarah finally asked. "This is all very painful for me."

"Because I want to know as much about you as possible," I said. "We're beginning a relationship with one another. How can I truly help you if I don't know you, *really* know you?"

"Well, yes," she said. "I'm sure I'll enjoy knowing you, but all this is considerably more than I expected."

"What did you expect?" I asked.

"Well, this is all new for me," she said in a halting voice, her lips trembling. "Paul always handled this sort of thing. I suppose I never realized how much was involved in keeping up a house. I thought it was only a matter of you coming by here, assessing the situation, giving me some sort of estimate, and then getting down to work."

"Estimate? What you need?" I asked in perplexity. "I don't know what you need until we talk, until you tell me."

"But that's *your* job, not mine," she said with some indignation. "Look around. Isn't it obvious to you?"

Then, with a look of suddenly dawning, shocked recognition, she said, "Wait a minute. You're the new preacher! I thought you were the house painter. I've been waiting all week for the man to give me an estimate on painting the house. I get it; you're the preacher, not the painter!"

The Christian Ministry,
July–August 1992

Part Four

Secrets

The secrets of the kingdom of heaven...
Those who have will receive more...
Changed hearts and lives will be healed...

70

Never Let You Go

She worked in the building where I worked. I didn't know her that well, but I enjoyed chatting with her when we occasionally ran into one another at the coffee bar.

"How are you doing?" I asked her.

"Okay," she said. "We've gone through a tough time. Our son stormed out one night in a rage. We didn't know if he was dead or alive for the past three months. Last night when my husband and I were having dinner, suddenly the front door burst open and in bursts our son, curses coming out of his mouth.

"'Thank God you're home!'" I said. "'Please, sit down and I'll fix you whatever you want for supper.'

"My son stomped through and headed down the hall to his room. He slammed the door and we heard him lock it. My husband does what he always does. He folded his napkin and silently got up from the dinner table, went into the den, and turned on the TV.

"I sat there and prayed, 'Lord, show me your way. Help me know what to do.' And it was just like Jesus told me to get up and walk down the hall and out to the garage to my husband's workshop. I looked on the workbench and immediately my eyes fell upon his biggest hammer. I picked it up and walked back in the house, back down the hall, and stood before the door to my son's room.

"'Son, I just want to talk. Please unlock the door.' He shouted curses from inside the bedroom. But it was like—it was like Jesus was guiding me. I drew back that hammer and came down with a strength not my own on the doorknob. In one blow I knocked off the whole doorknob and lock. Just split the door from top to bottom. What was left of the door swung open. There was my son, sitting on the bed, terrified.

"I lunged at him, 'I went into labor for you! I will never, ever let you go. Understand?

"'I think we are on a different footing.'"

I believe God is just like that.

71

A Helping Hand

An old man in a wrinkled, dirty suit shuffled up to Stephen. "Can you tell me where we're all headed? Kids blowin' themselves up in schools, oil spills, the end of Goldman Sachs, and what else? In God's name, what else?"

Stephen stood up and offered his hand to the disheveled old man. He asked solicitously, "Can I help?"

"You can if you have got some answers without bullshit," replied the drunk, burping and swaying as he spoke.

"Let me see if I can give you help," said Stephen. "Do you want some help?"

"Sure. Who don't?"

With that Stephen flipped open his cell phone, did a quick web search, and was relieved to discover an address for the Helping Hands Alcohol Information Center. It couldn't be more than a couple of blocks down the next street. *Thank you, Lord.*

"Let's walk together. I've got some people who can help you," said Stephen to the drunk.

The man narrowed his gaze, peered intently into Stephen's face, quizzically, and with a touch of apprehension, but he docilely allowed Stephen to lead him through the cluster of tables at the café and toward the corner. When they got to the intersection, the man started and said, "Wait a minute. What the... Do I know you? Where are you tryin' to take me?"

"A place where there are people who know how to help people with your sort of problems," Stephen said in his most reassuring, pastoral voice.

"What problems? They know where we're headed? You are the one with a problem!" said the man, wrenching his arm away from Stephen's grasp. "Who are you, anyway?" His voice rose. "You don't even know where we're headed! What the devil do you want to do with me? Help me, my ass!"

Terror spread over the man's face. As the streetlight changed and Stephen attempted to guide him across the street, the old man began to pull away. He dug in his heels as he shouted at the passersby, "Help! I don't even know this guy! He is trying to take me somewhere I don't want to go. Help! I'm being used!"

Stephen pulled him toward the street and into the crosswalk, re-straining the man from breaking free as he smiled to the people who stopped and stared. Because it was a nice, warm morning, Providence had provided for the maximum number of persons strolling down the street with all the time in the world to stop and gawk. Stephen mum-bled to the onlookers, "I'm trying to help this man. I'm a minister." He showed them his best attempt at a sanctimonious smile. "I work at Hope Church."

"Why should I give a damn where you work? Does that make right what you are doing to me?" shouted the old man, "Let go!" By the time Stephen had pulled him to the other side, the light had changed, traffic was moving into the crosswalk, and the man was whooping at the top of his voice, "Help! I don't even know this kid. He's taking advantage of me. Sweet Jesus!"

Stephen was mortified, hoping that no one would attempt a rescue of the shouting old drunk. Stephen smiled at the people on the street, most of whom were smiling back. Some were laughing at him as he coaxed and pulled the old man down the street toward the alcohol help center.

"I'm doing an intervention," he explained to one curious woman. "I'm a pastor. I'm trained."

Midway down the next block, the struggling old man, gritting his teeth and pulling against Stephen's urging, socked Stephen hard in his right side.

"Hey! Stop that," ordered Stephen. "That hurt."

"You're damn right, and I meant it, you jerk," hissed the old man.

For a man in his sad condition, he was surprisingly strong, thought Stephen as he urged him another fifty feet. By the next corner the man had ceased shouting and struggling, thank goodness, and was plodding along next to Stephen as if he had finally realized resistance was futile and he was doomed to be helped. Stephen was relieved when they at last reached their goal, building 3487, and he read the small sign, HELP-ING HANDS CENTER. Unfortunately, the sign also said, "Third Floor, Suite Two."

With one arm Stephen pushed through the revolving door. With his other arm he pulled the staggering, stumbling, wheezing man into the moving door with him. Stuck, even for a moment, in the door chamber with the old drunk made Stephen reel from the odor.

In the lobby, when a neatly dressed older woman exited the elevator, the man called out to her plaintively, "Madam, can you help a poor man? This black guy is trying to take me to a place I don't know where. For the love of God, get the police or somethin'. Help!"

When the lady paused and looked at the two of them, Stephen only said, "I'm a minister" and smiled. The lady moved quickly on and out of the lobby.

"That's the trouble with this country," mumbled the man. "Nobody wants to take responsibility."

Stephen then pulled the man into the elevator, with one hand pushed the button for the third floor, with the other he gripped the old man's arm, and prayed that he could endure the stench while they ascended.

The Helping Hands Center was a secretary seated behind a desk. When Stephen swung open the door, shoving the old man in before her, she jumped back in her chair and looked terrified. This suggested that though she had an assortment of pamphlets on her desk—"When Someone You Love is Addicted," and "The First Step in Recovery Is Asking for Help"—this was the first time the woman had ever actually come face-to-face with a street drunk.

Breathlessly, as he held on to the man's collar with one hand and gestured with the other, Stephen explained, "This brother would like some help with his problem. I met him on the street, just a couple of blocks away, and have brought him here for you to help. I'm a minister. I'm Stephen."

"How did you get up here? We are an alcohol information center," the woman responded. "We give out information, pamphlets, things of that nature. We don't do treatment. I don't know who told you to come here."

"But, I, er, what can I do with him?" he asked.

"Hey lady, I'll take some information," the old man said, looking at the woman, giving her a toothless smile. "I'd like one of them pamphlets you got. I got into this mess with this black kid just tryin' to get information."

She thrust "Resources for Recovery" at him and quickly resumed her place of safety behind the desk.

"Well, what can we do?" Stephen asked. "It was all I could do to get him in here. We've got to help."

"I'm here by myself," said the woman, in a terrified voice. "We're informational rather than therapeutic. I'll have to go downstairs and ask Mr. Gunderson what we can do. You cannot leave that man here. We've never..." With that she grabbed her purse and keys, slipped sideways from behind the desk, and carefully keeping her distance from Stephen and his ward, exited, disappearing when the elevator door opened.

"I'm worn-out," said the old man to Stephen. "I got to sit down. You have next to killed me with your god-awful tryin' to help me. My mistake was to ask you anything, damn you."

Stephen guided the old man into a metal chair next to the desk and took a seat beside him, saying, "These people are professionals."

"You—you goddamn, know-it-all do-gooder, you! Did I ever ask you to take me to this place? Did I? This is America! I've got rights," slurred the man. "We've got a Constertushun and the last time I checked, it still meant somethin'. Fool."

Within just a moment after this philosophical/prophetic outburst, the old man passed out, mouth gaping open, sort of snoring as he slumped over in his chair, saliva dripping down the left side of his chin.

Stephen sat next to him for another few moments, trying to keep the old man from falling out of his chair, and (because he was working for Jesus) allowing the stench to waft over him, feeling nauseated but also righteous. He was discovering that it was all well and good to speak of ministry as reaching out to those in need; it was otherwise actually to have close contact with the wretched of the earth. Sitting there, sick from the smell and the wheezing, Stephen admitted to himself that if he couldn't actually do some good for someone in pain, he couldn't stand to be around them. That this old man was beyond help, and had no desire to be helped, exposed the limits of Stephen's ability to be in Christian ministry. He despised the old man for his rebuke.

Ever so carefully rising, Stephen regained his professional composure. A drunk had sobered him up. He quietly stood up, tiptoed out, softly closing the door to Helping Hands Alcohol Information Center, then raced down the hall, hitting the steel door to the stairwell with a bang, bounded down the three flights of steps like an agile gazelle, exited into the street, and walked briskly—no, ran—without looking back, down the sidewalk, dashing breathlessly and putting as much distance between himself and the drunk's reproachful, unassuageable need as possible.

Incorporation: A Novel,
Wipf and Stock Publishers, 2012

72

Unto Us a Child

It had been a long, frustrating wait: the tests, the treatments, the discouragement, the unknowing. We wanted a child. But we were learning that a child is one blessing that is a gift—unearned, unachieved, undemanded. "We know more about how to help couples not have children than how to help them have children," the doctor had said.

But at last the hoped-for, prayed-for dream became reality. The gynecologist, who in today's upside-down world had spent his day helping people avoid pregnancy, gave my wife the news.

Through the fall, she grew "great with child," as Matthew or Luke would have said. As the December days grew short and cold, we watched this mystery of mysteries unfold.

Patsy said that she knew the Christmas cantata was not written for our child, but as our little church choir struggled through John Peterson's maudlin *Love Transcending*, sometimes she caught herself singing for our child, growing in her womb, rather than for Mary's baby. And on the night of the cantata, when she processed with the choir, she knew that she was on her way to Bethlehem. As the lector spoke of Mary's being "blessed among women," Patsy said Gabriel was speaking to her. And we rejoiced, like Elizabeth and Mary before us, when they had talked about the advent of their babies.

That December, we found that there is no better time to be waiting for a child than Advent, when the whole world waits for a baby.

A few years ago, a preacher friend of mine chided us for our seasonal, sentimental infatuation with the baby Jesus. He urged us to think less about the sweet baby Jesus and more about the grown-up Christ. I agreed with him at the time (so much so that I preached his sermon with good effect, on more than one occasion!). But today I know more than I knew then. Now I find myself, as the International Year of the Child comes to an end and the season of the Babe at Bethlehem is here, prodded by a second reading of Raymond Brown's *Birth of the Messiah*; and I think again about the advent of our baby—and Mary's.

I know the dangers of our annual attempt to reduce the majesty of the incarnation at Bethlehem in Judea to cute, infantile, manageable proportions here in our living-room crèche in Durham, North Carolina. I'll admit to the sentimental mush of "Away in a Manger" and its theologically questionable cooing over the "little Lord Jesus." But now I know also, from firsthand experience of no more than three Advents ago, how threatening babies are.

Herod knew. King Herod, the old fox, sitting in Jerusalem, with all the military clout of the empire to back him up, knew how *dangerous* babies can be. Herod knew that he had better take matters into his own hands while he still had time, before the child could mock the impotence of the old man. It was no time to wait for the unknown, potential, growing child to come to fulfillment. With babies, Herod knew, the unknown both attracts and repels.

We fear childish impudence and disrespect in the face of our adult pompousness. The Central African Empire's Emperor Bokassa knew this when he reenacted the Massacre of the Innocents after some impudent schoolchildren refused to wear his silly, state-imposed uniforms. I have found it is difficult to retain my delusions of adult authority and omnipotence when the wee one across the breakfast table sends the cereal flying in my direction and then laughs at how funny I look with oatmeal on my suit. Every baby challenges Herod's, Bokassa's, and my claims of power and immortality. The future is that child's, not mine, not yours. With each passing day, we decrease; they increase. Is that why we waver between the extremes of romantic glorification of childhood on the one hand and toleration of child abuse and child neglect on the other?

I know that a baby is supposed to bring out the best in us. But never forget that a baby mirrors the worst also. Why did Patsy and I so desperately want a baby? To make secure our claim of immortality in a mortal world? To reap security for our old age in an insecure time? To achieve vicarious fulfillment by living out what we regret from our past through our parental plans for her future? Like all human creations, even the creation of a child is tinged with our subtle, deceptive human pride.

And why did Judea want a baby—this child Messiah? To bring us the gift of immorality through his entrance into our mortal flesh? To offer us self-fulfillment by championing our causes and choosing us, and us alone, for the benefits of his love? To promise us eternal security and peace that frees us from earthly insecurity? The Advent of the Christ child, like all of God's incarnations, was impossible without his advent into the realm of our subtle, deceptive, human pride—into the realm of all our ambivalent expectations.

There, in the baby, "the hopes and fears of all the years" are met by a God who meets us where we live—with our subtle pride masquerading as faith, with our false hopes and selfish fears—and claims us at that infantile point where each of us began our meandering life journey. Starting at the beginning, darkest fears, recreating our humanity from the womb onward.

But even this does not adequately describe the mystery we sense at seeing God in the manger. The most disturbing quality of the baby Jesus, the mystery of his advent that scandalizes even as it inexorably beckons, is the vulnerability of his incarnation.

Nothing is so helpless, so dependent, so fragile, so frail as a baby. I know of no other religion so bold as to admit to the possibility of its God appearing in so vulnerable a form. How scandalously conde-scending is the love of this God who deems to meet us first as a baby. How threatening to my human desire for an aloof, Platonic deity who lives in the realm of the abstract, self-contained ideal, rather than in the stable out back, wrapped in swaddling clothes and lying in a manger. For most of the year we preach about humanity's need for God. But on Christmas, can we be so bold as to speak of God's freely chosen need for humanity—a God who comes, reaching out to us, as a baby, needing the love, warmth, and nurture of an utterly human family?

I have noted that within some of the rituals and festivals of churches in impoverished nations, great prominence is given to the infant Christ. An old man in a poor Italian village first explained this to me as we stood one December in his little church before an altar crèche and "il Santo Bambino."

"Il bambino," he said, whispering to me in toothless solemnity, "is poor, little, and outside—like us." Then he smiled.

Not too far up the road from this old man's town, Francis of Assisi had done much reflection upon the Holy Child, seeing the Babe as a paradigm for God's suffering servanthood among the poor of God's earth. Perhaps we more powerful ones can do no better than to sentimentalize and trivialize this fragile Babe. Maybe God leaves to the poor, to the out-siders, to the "little ones" of the world to see the powerful, revolutionary, messianic, divine-human solidarity that the presence of the Babe declares.

And with the vulnerability of the Babe comes also his claim upon us. A baby, because of its vulnerability, dependency, and potential, evokes a response from us, demands a commitment unknown in the majority of human encounters. This claim arises not only because babies need us but also because, somewhere within our deepest selves, we know that we need babies. Our belly button tells so many fundamental truths about our true situation. Some deep, human instinct tells us that babies are a sign of our human creativity at its best, a reminder of our dark, biologi-cal, primordial origins in the waters of creation, and a hopeful hint of our still-open future. Call it life. One finds it difficult to be neutral in the face of such smiling mystery.

A parishioner once explained it to me this way: He had interpreted and kept his marriage vows rather loosely, had thought little about his past and had not the slightest interest in the future. He had spent the first years of his marriage mainly on the road, making money.

"But one night," he said, "I got turned around—the night I walked into the hospital room and held my little baby in my arms for the first time and realized that she was part of me even if she was better than I deserved. I said to myself, 'You're going to have to stop your foolishness and start living like somebody, because she's somebody.'"

The birth of that baby summoned forth the best in the man's humanity, laid hold of his life in a manner that could only be called rebirth.

Did Joseph and Mary feel such a claim upon their lives as they stood by the manger, or did the shepherds and the magi? And what is that wonder that we feel reflected back upon us when we encounter the Babe? Is it a glimpse of ourselves at our best, in our primal innocence? Or is it a vision of One who is part of us, yet better than we deserve? Who are these fortunate somebodies who stand around the manger, blessed by so close a love? Who could expect the magi to return home the same way after such a meeting?

This December, if a messenger in white—whether a gynecologist or the angel Gabriel—should tell you that you were blessed and that you were going to be given a baby, I hope you would sing as Mary sang. You could spend your Advent wait in less productive, less creative ways, I can assure you. Waiting, you might discover firsthand the truth of God's incarnation among us.

As for me, I know I'm supposed to keep my categories clean, and carefully define the limits between the divine and the human. But God help me, I know that while I may be singing about the baby Jesus this season, I'll always be seeing baby Harriet—that little one who, now in the third Advent of her life, stands before me, demanding that I put aside my pen and tell her a bedtime story, as she and I wait in the December darkness for the God who came first as a child. And so I begin: "Once there was a woman named Mary, and she was told that she was going to have a baby…"

The Christian Century,
December 19, 1979

73

Hearsay

They said they had heard of Methodists but had never seen one until the circuit rider showed up and started holding meetings under the brush arbor next to Smith's pasture. He was loud once he got to preaching.

Three of them, and one a confirmed tippler, got saved that week, so they said, "Maybe we ought to start a church."

They met every Sunday for three months—at the brush arbor on good days, in Thomas's barn when it rained. They shared three Methodist hymnals and two Bibles among themselves.

The circuit rider came back to town the next May and told them, "Ya'll need to build you a proper church."

They got together and bought a piece of property down by the creek. By September, they started to build. Annie Johnson's egg money bought the first lumber.

The next Easter they worshipped for the first time in the new church. Thirty people by now. The circuit rider wasn't there because he had been thrown from his horse last January.

They said, "Let's put in a well." Then came the cemetery when Brother James died. Next, the little Lester baby.

On the tenth anniversary, they built a nice little building to the side for Sunday school. "Twenty children! Who'd have believed it?"

They said, "Pews built in Nashville, hymnals from the Publishing House... let's have a fall revival meeting."

Souls were harvested. That year they were put on a two-point circuit with worship at one o'clock every Sunday.

They said, "Someday before long we'll be a station church and have our own pastor."

When the mill opened, four new families moved to town and joined the church.

They said, "We never had a seminary-trained preacher before. But we're willing to try."

"Birthplace of Methodism in Lee County," said the sign out front.

They said, "It's about time we got air conditioning. We're no longer a country church." George and Mable Watson gave a nice electric organ in memory of George Jr., who died in the war.

"Today, our membership has risen to almost three hundred, not counting the children," the lay leader proudly announced. "Second largest in this part of the state. All our apportionments paid in full."

They said, "Preacher, are you sure those folks would be happy in our church? Wouldn't it be better for them to find a church that would be more suited for people like them?"

"I don't care what the *Book of Discipline* says; we're just not used to change. We're not ready for this," said the chair of the board.

They said, "That preacher never did seem to be a good fit. I hope the bishop will send us somebody who can love us and this church."

"If that's the best you can do for the pastor's salary," said the bishop, "my choices for your next preacher are limited."

They said, "This church has a proud history and a beautiful building. We're not growing; still, we are holding our own."

"Although we are small, we are a loving, caring community of people," said the newest pastor, a student from the seminary. "Although this is now just a part-time appointment, we love one another."

Last day, they said to the district superintendent, "Here's the keys to the padlock on the front door. This church has lots of memories. Nobody's fault. Lot of love passed through this church. It's a shame."

74

Great Moments in Worship

I used to tell students that I was working on a book called *The Ten Worst Moments in the History of Liturgy*. Alternative title: *Ten Worship Services Jesus Would Have Walked Out Of*. The students would bring me examples to consider for my top-ten list. I noted that most of their nominations involved children's sermons—a liturgical practice not dear to my heart. (However, when I wrote an article questioning the use of trite children's sermonettes, I received nearly as much negative mail as I did when I criticized racist Christian schools. So, if you love to do children's sermons, just do them as best you can, and don't write me about it.)

After Easter one year, a student gave me this case study in liturgics for my best of the worst list:

My field assignment is at this large church in a town near here. We have this young associate minister who is always trying something new. (He thinks he knows everything.) Well, on Holy Saturday I went by the church to check on a few things, and there was the associate, hard at work on something in the corner of the sanctuary. He was hammering away at what looked like a small stage set made out of plywood and papier-mâché. With fear and trembling, I asked him what he was doing.

"Have you ever read *The Velveteen Rabbit*?" he asked.

"Yes," I said. "It's a children's book, isn't it?"

"Precisely! So, when it comes time for the Children's Moment tomorrow, I'm going to call the kids down front and read the Easter story. Then I'm going to read from *The Velveteen Rabbit*. I've got this stuffed rabbit here, and I am going to shove it in this hole in my papier-mâché tomb, like this."

With that, he stuffed the toy rabbit in his tomb.

"Then," he continued, "I'm going to count to three and pull out a live bunny rabbit from the tomb. Get it? Resurrection!"

"Does the pastor know that you are planning this?" I asked.

"No, not yet," he replied, "But won't he be surprised!"

"Yes, surprised—or something like that," I said. I stumbled out of the sanctuary, not knowing what to do. I decided to go over to the pastor's house, just across the yard. The pastor's wife met me at the door. Unfortunately, she said, her husband was up in Raleigh visiting a sick parishioner.

"I'm afraid that he will be the one who's really sick after tomorrow's service," I said. She asked me what was wrong. I felt I had to tell her. I described the tomb, the stuffed rabbit, and the live bunny. The pastor's wife stood there for a moment. Then she gritted her teeth and said, "I want you to go right back over there and tell that nincompoop that I am speaking for my husband when I say to get those damn rabbits—stuffed or unstuffed—and that papier-mâché tomb out of the church, or he will have to be resurrected in order to serve a church ever again!"

Liturgical innovation postponed.

The Christian Ministry, March 1987

75

Before Us Good People

Take my first congregation. Please. Rural Georgia (rural doesn't get more rural). I, fresh from Yale Divinity School, Bultmanned-Tilliched-and-Barthed-up for grad school at Emory. Saturday before my first Sunday, I drove out to survey my assignment—misnamed Friendship Methodist Church. A large padlock hung from the front door.

The lay leader—who laid carpet in Smyrna—explained the padlock with, "After that there prayer meeting went bad, people was ripping pews out of the floor, carting off memorial gifts they had given. So, the sheriff come out and put on that there chain until the new preacher could come and talk some sense into them."

Standing in the gray dust of the hot gravel parking lot, I thought, *I wanted to be William Sloane Coffin preaching to Christianity's cultured despisers, and the director of field work at Candler made me Margaret Mead, stunned by the primitive puberty rites of Samoans.*

My days there were typified by squabbling, disappointment followed by undeniable failure, fornication between an alleged soprano and a bogus baritone after choir practice, the father of the bride and the father of the groom duking it out in the parking lot before a wedding.

When people asked, "Where is your church?" I replied, "Thirty miles and two centuries from Atlanta."

One day, in youthful despair, I poured out my frustration on a favorite Emory professor.

Dr. Hunter sympathetically listened—fisticuffs in the parking lot, choral cuckoldry. He agreed to the injustice of someone as talented as I forced to serve such losers as they.

"Worst of all," Hunter said, grinning, "Jesus says those whores and tax collectors get to go into the kingdom of God before us good people.

"What are people like us going to do in heaven?"

What's Right with the Church, Insight, 1998

76

Easter Proof

I had seen him on Sundays at the chapel, so I invited him over to the house, where I made him a sandwich and we had lunch on the patio.

"So, tell me about yourself," I said.

"Well, I was a teenager from hell, made my parents' lives miserable," he began.

"We hear that story a lot around here. Nothing special in that," I said.

"I was so bad they had me committed to a mental institution for teenagers," he continued.

"Can you do that?" I asked.

"I broke out of that place, hitchhiked to Chicago, where I lived on the streets as a prostitute. One night I rolled this guy, a businessman from out of town, took his wallet, and went on a spree with his credit cards until the cops got me and I was sent to Joliet for three years."

"Wow. I thought you meant that you did some stuff with cheerleaders in high school," I responded in wonder.

"I told you I was bad. Don't know if you have ever been in a prison like that, but it was hell. I had hit bottom. This older prisoner took me under his wing, would read to me from the Bible at night before lockdown. He was the worst reader. Took him forever to get through a chapter, but I grew up a Catholic; I didn't know much about the Bible. So, one night he was reading from the Gospel of Luke, I think it was that section about the lost sheep, lost coin, and the prodigal son. And it was just like Jesus himself walked into that cell and grabbed me, slammed me against the wall, and said to me, 'I got plans for you. Now, cut this shit out!'"

"Wow. We don't hear stories like yours very often."

"So, I got my high school degree, got out of Joliet, went to Michigan State and made straight As, but I always wanted to go to Duke," he said, "so I transferred here, and I've done great with my grades."

"Wow."

"Here's my point," he continued as he finished his sandwich. "You're a preacher, right? And I bet you preachers are always looking around for good stories to use in your sermons. We've got Easter coming up. Can't be easy to preach the Resurrection at a place like Duke. *I am your proof Easter is true.*"

A Peculiar Prophet: William H.
Willimon and the Art of Preaching,
Abingdon Press, 2004

77

The Joy of Being a Sinner

He was a Duke MD/PhD student. Very smart. Each year, only one or two earn both those degrees at once.

"What have you learned since you have been in the Duke Medical Center?" I asked.

He replied, "You would be interested to know that I've learned that nobody should practice medicine who is not a Missouri Synod Lutheran."

What?

"Know much about Missouri Synod Lutherans?" he asked.

"I know they're conservative, a bit standoffish. Your pastors don't come to the local ministerial association meetings. I know that," I replied.

"The main thing about my church is that we are big on sin. That's mostly what our preachers preach. They tell us that we sin before we are saved and after we are saved. In fact, the only way that you can be damned, as a Missouri Synod Lutheran, is to think that you might not be damned."

What?

"I had never been around people who thought they were good until I came to Duke. So, I had never known anybody who didn't know how to confess sin," he continued. "Here in the hospital, when a patient dies after surgery, we hold a morbidity and mortality meeting. We discuss the case, what went wrong. And you wouldn't believe how defensive everybody is.

"'We followed proper protocol,' they say. 'We used the best procedures that are followed by the most elite medical schools in the country,' they declare. 'The surgery went just as planned.'

"'But, er, uh, the patient *died*,' I say, in the humblest way I can.

"'That can't be blamed on us!' they snap back. Proper protocol. Best procedures. Just as planned.

"'But we didn't plan for the patient to expire, did we?' I ask.

"So, every morning, as I walk in the Duke Medical Center, I look over that vast array of buildings and say a little prayer: 'Lord, a lot of good will be done here today, but some bad too. And we won't know we've screwed up until afterwards, when there's no way to put it right. Forgive us, Lord, sinners as we are. Amen.'

"So grateful to be a Missouri Synod Lutheran."

Pastor: The Theology and Practice of
Ordained Ministry, Abingdon Press, 2002

78
Olympics for Clerics

Picture yourself on a Sunday in the middle of the church service. With considerable flourish, you have just announced that you are going to baptize a baby. The child's proud parents and godparents bring the infant forward while the congregation smiles. Two hundred pairs of eyes are on you as you put aside your worship book, lift the lid off the font, and, to your horror, find that it is empty, bone-dry, as desiccated as the Sahara.

Preserving your pleasant, unruffled, official clerical smile, you look up and say in a clear, resonant voice, "And now, Jane Jones, our chairperson of the worship committee, will obtain *the water.*"

Jones casts her eyes from right to left, then, somewhat hesitantly, moves from her seat. Reassured by your nod, smile, and confidence, she leaves the sanctuary, runs to the church kitchen, gets a pitcher, goes to the women's room, fills the pitcher with water, returns, and hands it to you. As you take it, you ask the congregation to bow while you say a short prayer that thanks God for the "freshness of water."

The parents, godparents, and congregation participate in the succeeding ritual with no apparent awareness that anything was amiss. In fact, a number of people in the congregation whisper their approval of this thoughtful addition to the Service of Christian Baptism.

Then, to the rear of the church, five people stand up, each holding a large white card reading, respectively, 4, 5, 4, 4, 5—a near-perfect score for a nearly faultless performance in a tough ecclesial situation. You have taken the lead in the Emergency Liturgical Adaptation competition.

This stirring spectacle was recently enacted in Pasadena, California, at the First Clergy Olympiad, sponsored by the Greater Pasadena Council of Churches. It is the brainchild of the Rev. Dr. John Winterbottom, who, inspired by the 1984 Olympics to be held in Los Angeles, organized this gathering of the nation's best pastors.

"It all started with a dream," said Winterbottom. "I was home one night, eating tacos with my wife and kids, when I received this inspiration. I said to myself, 'How come we preachers never get a chance to show just how good we are at what we do?' The average person has no idea of the demands of the parish ministry, the kinds of pressures we are under, the heroic acts that we do every day, without congregational recognition, and for meager salaries and short vacations."

This set Winterbottom on his way to founding the Clergy Olympiad. "We needed some way to recognize and improve the work that pastors do. This event is our way of saying, 'Hey, world, these guys and gals know what they're doing and they are damn good at it.'"

Clergy from nearly thirty states were present for the beginning of the four-day competition. Most of the participants were Protestant, with evangelicals having the largest representation and taking the most gold medals. Though the event failed to win the official approval of the Vatican, a number of Roman Catholic observers attended this year's games.

"You really get to see the quality of the work that's being done out there in the field," said one layperson from Ventura. "There are some real professionals here. I've noted that the evangelicals seem to have it over the liberals. I think that they are a little more competitive, a little less prone to 'turn the other cheek' as far as professional competition goes. Real hot shots."

While space limitations prohibit describing all aspects of the Olympiad in detail, here are a few of the highlights. Jane Smith, though in her late thirties, easily won the calling-card dash. In this event, participants must run from their parked automobiles up a seventy-foot walkway, ring a doorbell, leave their calling cards tucked firmly in the door, and get back into their cars before the inhabitants have time to answer the bell.

Smith, a Presbyterian from Kansas, said that she entered the ministry comparatively late in life. This makes her performance in this event particularly noteworthy. "I serve a rather large parish," she explained. "And being a woman, I have to work just a little bit harder than most men in order to prove myself." She had no trouble besting her male competitors in this event. "And because of my denomination, I had to sprint through this event in heels," Smith boasted.

As was to be expected, Episcopalians dominated the field in liturgical contests such as the rapid recitation of the Eucharist.

United Methodists made a surprisingly good showing in the confirmation marathon, a grueling, nonstop endurance test in which a pastor has to give three lectures on history, doctrine, and polity to a group of fifth and sixth graders. Since confirmation is a comparatively recent phenomenon among United Methodists, their superb performance clearly caught the Lutherans and Episcopalians off guard. "Well, they have less history, doctrine, and polity than we do," commented a disgruntled member of the losing, Lutheran team. "Besides, our kids are less well-behaved than Methodists."

The potluck relay required pastors to hurry down the serving line of a typical potluck dinner, heaping their plates with at least ten items while avoiding Swedish meatballs and tuna surprise.

The event that everyone in the crowd most eagerly awaited was the clergy decathlon. This contest lumped together a score of torturous, demanding clerical skills in a two-hour trial of endurance. Perhaps because of their belief in economic competition and in the body as a temple, the evangelicals took the field here. The Methodists looked good in the first event—filling out year-end reports, an area in which Baptists clearly had little experience.

As was expected, Baptists, Methodists, and Presbyterians fell behind in the liturgical-vesting competition. For the UCCs, this event was an expected but still humiliating defeat.

The two UCC competitors from Wisconsin dropped hopelessly behind when they were unable to tell the front from the back of a damask chasuble.

"Like we give a rip about lace and brocade," said a UCC-er. "Justice ministry is my bag."

By the time the decathlon moved into the preaching-volume-throw and the tedious member-vault, Baptists commanded an easy lead. Although they stumbled in the doctrinal-disagreement hurdles, these more conservative pastors had smooth sailing through the rest of the decathlon.

"While we *believe* in salvation by grace alone, we owe it all to practice, practice, practice," said Fred Walker of Macedonia Baptist in Little Rock.

All in all, it was a wonderful ecumenical occasion. Participants went away with a better appreciation of each other's cultural and theological differences and similarities. Spectators were unanimous in their praise for the pastors.

"I just never knew that being a pastor was so tough," said an observing seminarian from Melodyland. "I'm going back to my studies with a new sense of dedication. Who knows? Maybe someday I'll be the first Pentecostal to take a gold medal in the doctrinal-disagreement hurdles."

"Wow. These guys are the best in the business," said an astonished layman. "I thought they went to seminary because they couldn't get into law school. What did I know? I watched a pastor terminate a talk by a visiting Gideon in only three minutes. Wow."

Such comments made all the struggle, hard work, and derision worthwhile to Dr. Winterbottom. Said Winterbottom, "Right now, out in Iowa or someplace like that, some unknown, unheralded pastor is going about his or her duties, dreaming of the time when he or she will be good enough to compete with the greats at the Clergy Olympiad II. Maybe that dream will keep that pastor going."

The next Olympiad is scheduled to be held in either Nashville, Tennessee, or Tulsa, Oklahoma.

The Christian Century,
November 23, 1983

79

Best Little Harlot's House in Jericho

By faith Rahab the prostitute wasn't killed with the disobedient because she welcomed the spies in peace.

Hebrews 11:31

Shocking, in the midst of the traditional epistle lesson for All Saints, to come across the name of one engaged in a most unsaintly profession: Rahab the harlot. How dare the writer of Hebrews include this woman of ill repute in so noble a list of God's saints? Abel, Noah, Abraham, Sarah, Moses—yes. But Rahab? Sure, "Rahab the Sunday school teacher," or "Rahab the missionary" or "Rahab the president of the United Methodist Women" among the saints, but Rahab the harlot?

Somehow Rahab got mentioned in an even more surprising context. In Matthew's genealogy of Jesus's forebears, there she is (Matt 1:5). Rahab, wife of Salmon, mother of Boaz, great-great-great-grandmama of our Lord himself.

It's enough to make you think. If a harlot can be a saint, anybody can.

Backstory: Joshua led the hosts of Israel to the threshold of the promised land. Two spies were sent to reconnoiter the situation in Jericho. They ended up at Rahab's place, in a seedy section of town, perhaps forgetting that they were on a military mission, not on a weekend bash at the NCO Club.

The king got word that spies were roving about and sent messengers to seize them. When they inquired at Rahab's place, she protected the spies with a lie.

"Of course," she said, "the men came to me. But I didn't know where they were from. The men left when it was time to close the gate at dark, but I don't know where the men went. Hurry! Chase after them! You might catch up with them" (Josh 2:4-5). The king's men rushed on, not knowing that Rahab had stashed the Israelites in stalks of flax on the roof.

Rahab told the spies that she had heard of the mighty works of their God and had enough sense to know that "the LORD your God is God in heaven above and on earth below" (Josh 2:11). All she asked of the Israelites was that they show her family mercy when the walls came tumbling down in Jericho.

Then, while it was still night, the crafty Rahab let them down by a rope through the window, tying a scarlet thread there to identify her place for the invading Israelites. When Joshua and his army finally entered the city, they led Rahab and her people out to safety. The people of the red-thread house in the red-light district were the only ones spared when the invaders leveled Jericho.

Harlot, liar—what a seedy sort of saint. And yet, to be fair, Rahab was not alone in her seediness. Poor, drunken, naked Noah; desert sheik Abraham with his squabbling family; old, conniving Sarah; hot-headed Moses the murderer; lustful David; cowardly Peter; bigoted Paul—the stories the Bible tells of God's saints compose a rogues' gallery if ever there were one. If people like them can be saints, anybody can.

Who is a "saint"? Israel is called a nation of saints: "You are a people holy to the LORD your God. You are the ones whom the LORD selected to be his own, to be a treasured people out of all other people on earth" (Deut 14:2). Why choose Israel? Perhaps because Israel was more religious than other ancient nations, more pious, more sanctified? No. The Bible is clear: "It was not because you were greater than all other people that the LORD loved you and chose you. In fact, you were the smallest of peoples! No, it is because the LORD loved you" (Deut 7:7-8).

It was out of love that God chose Israel. "The smallest of peoples" became great because of God's choice. The biblical writers bend over backwards to make this point clear. It was not due to any attribute or achievement on Israel's part that she was chosen. Israel would play the harlot before and after her election. Waywardness, infidelity, idolatry, nationalism, pride, and lechery were just a few of the sins charged to Israel's account before the story's end. Whatever is meant by "a people holy to the Lord," it means something other than a people pure, spotless, and blameless.

Biblical saintliness is first a matter of what God does with people rather than what they do for God. A person is called "saint" in the Bible because God wants him or her to do something holy, not because that person's special character merits notice by God. Saints are people who are called by God to participate in God's work.

As Karl Barth says in *The Christian Life* a person is sanctified in the Bible when that person is "dedicated to the service of God" by God's "separation, claiming, commandeering, and preparation" of one for divine service. That is what happened to Rahab. On a typical day, going about her typical business, the old girl got commandeered for God. Hers was an experience not unknown to other ordinary folk like Abel, Noah, Abraham, Sarah, and Moses. Their saintliness lay in their chosenness.

"You are a chosen race, a royal priesthood, a holy nation," declares 1 Peter 2:9 to the first Christians. They are chosen because God's got work for them to do: to "speak of the wonderful acts of the one who called you out of darkness into his amazing light" (v. 9b). They are chosen not because they have it made but because of God's loving decision to make something out of them: "Once you weren't a people, but now you are God's people" (v. 10). It is in this sense that the New Testament refers to the church as saints. Like Israel, out of a bunch of nobodies come somebodies.

On All Saints we remember the saints, all of them. It's not for you or me to pass judgment on God's judgments of who ought to do God's work. What looks like seediness to us often looks like potential for saintliness to God. There is some evidence for the notion that God passes over the nice, pure people because sweet, saintly people aren't always the ones to get the job done—especially when the jobs that need doing are as tough and demanding as the ones God takes on.

Although Rahab lacked in the area of conventional sexual morals, she was a survivor. She wasn't born yesterday. Rahab had been in business long enough to know how to take care of her own, and therefore proved quite helpful in looking after some of God's own.

Whom do you think about when you hear the word *saints*? Perhaps you think of some pious Sunday school teacher who taught you in the third grade. Perhaps your memory of this man or woman challenges the Rahab image of sainthood. But I submit that any person who is capable of running a third-grade Sunday school class without receiving or administering bodily injury and still is able to convert a few eight-year-old pagans along the way has got something more to commend her than sweetness and piousness.

This is how saints are made, not in long bouts of prayer and meditation, not in earnestly cultivating their spiritual side. Saints are made by listening to the call of God and saying *yes*.

Rahab was minding her own business, looking after things in her place, when the Lord, through two frightened spies, asked her to mind God's business. She said *yes*, and therefore is listed among the heroes and heroines of the faith. The letter from James says that Rahab got to be a saint by her good work (James 2:25). That's part of the story. But I think the author of Hebrews is more nearly correct in saying that it was by faith more than by good work that she entered sainthood—faith that God could use even a person like her.

On All Saints Day, let's remember the saints—all of them, including the odd ones, the good little bad boys among them, the unlikely, unsuspecting ones, the Rahabs, the Abrahams, the Sarahs, and all the rest, who lived and died, listened and responded, and thereby pointed the way for the rest of us. If they can be saints, anybody can. Anybody.

All you who are faithful, love the LORD!

The LORD protects those who are loyal. (Ps 31:23)

The Christian Century,
October 26, 1983

80

Bless You, Mrs. Degrafinried

Happy are people who make peace, because they will be called God's children.

Matthew 5:9

It all started early Tuesday morning, February 21, when Louise Degrafinried's husband, Nathan, got up from bed in Mason, Tennessee to let out the cat. "Cat," as they call him, stood at the edge of the porch, his hair bristled up on his arched back, and hissed.

"What you see out there, Cat?" Nathan asked as he squinted into the darkness.

A big man stepped from around the corner of the house and pointed a shotgun at Nathan.

"Lord, honey," Louise heard her husband shout. "Open the door! He's got a gun."

Before she could open the door, the man with the gun had shoved Nathan inside, pushing him and Louise against the wall.

"Don't make me kill you!" he shouted, thrusting the gun in their faces. The couple knew immediately that the intruder was one of the escaped inmates whom they had heard about on the radio. He was Riley Arzeneaux of Memphis, who, with four other inmates, had escaped from Fort Pillow State Prison the previous Saturday.

Louise Degrafinried, a seventy-three-year-old grandmother, stood her ground. "Young man," she said, "I am a Christian lady. I don't believe in no violence. Put that gun down and you sit down. I don't allow no violence here."

The man relaxed his grip on the shotgun. He looked at her for a moment. Then he laid his gun on the couch.

"Lady," he said quietly, "I'm so hungry. I haven't had nothing to eat for three days."

"Young man, you just sit down there and I'll fix you breakfast. Nathan," she said, "go get this young man some dry socks."

With that, Louise went to work. She fixed him bacon, eggs, white bread toast, milk, and coffee. Then she got out her best cloth napkins and set her kitchen table.

> "When we sat down, I took that young man by the hand and said, 'Young man, let's give thanks that you came here and that you are safe.' I said a prayer and then asked him if he would like to say something to the Lord. He didn't say anything, so I said, 'Just say, "Jesus wept."' Then we all ate breakfast."

> *"Why did you tell him to say, 'Jesus wept'?" I asked her later. "Because," she said, "I figured that he didn't have no church background, so I wanted to start him off simple; something short, you know."*

> "After breakfast, we sat there and I began to pray. Held his hand and kept patting him on the leg. He trembled all over. I said, 'Young man, I love you and God loves you. God

loves us all, every one of us, especially you. Jesus died for you because he loves you so much.'"

"'You sound just like my grandmother,' he said, 'She's dead.'" Nathan said that he saw a tear fall down the boy's cheek.

"About that time we heard police cars coming down the road. 'They gonna kill me when they get here,' he said.

"'No, young man, they aren't going to hurt you. You done wrong, but God loves you.' Then me and Nathan took him by the arms, helped him up, and took him out of the kitchen toward the door. 'Let me do all the talking,' I told him. The police got out of their cars. They had their guns out. I shouted to them, 'Y'all put those guns away. I don't allow no violence here. Put them away. This young man wants to go back.'

"'Nathan,' I said, you bring the young man on out to the car.' Then they put the handcuffs on him and took him back to the prison."

That afternoon, two of the prisoners, who had been separated from Arzeneaux earlier, entered a suburban backyard where a couple were barbecuing. The husband went into his house and came out with a gun. The escapees shot and killed him and took his wife hostage. They released her the next day.

Was Mrs. Degrafinried frightened? "No," she said. "Nathan said he was scared, but not me. I knew God was with me, that God had sent that young man to me for a reason. I knew God would lead me in the right direction."

Nathan and Louise Degrafinried are lifelong members of Mount Sinai Primitive Baptist Church. There, no doubt, they often sang the old hymn "Are Ye Able":

Are ye able to remember,

When a thief lifts up his eyes,

That his pardoned soul is worthy

Of a place in paradise?

Lord, we are able.

Our spirits are thine.

Remold them, make us,

Like thee, divine.

The Christian Century,
March 14, 1984

81

Partners in Ministry

If you are the guy who introduced me to Pat Robertson, please identify yourself. I have never met Pat, never have known a real live presidential candidate; still, that doesn't keep Pat from barraging me with monthly mailings and evening telephone calls asking for money. Even my in-laws wouldn't do that.

My relationship with Pat began in 1986 when I received a packet of tapes and pamphlets proclaiming that I had just joined Pat's "700 Club." The accompanying letter, personally signed by Pat, explained that my generous support was enabling the 700 Club TV program to reach millions of people every day. I also was helping to keep open a telephone line so that thousands of prayer requests could get through (4 million people called last year); to clothe and to feed millions of people through Operation Blessing; to sustain the CBN University; and to help "restore a biblical consensus to America." I would have felt great about that except that I had not given a dime to Pat. Someone else deserves the credit. Would you who sent in my name please identify yourself?

I really felt guilty when I received a gold 700 Club pin, a membership card, a copy of the Christian Broadcasting Network (CBN) Partnership Newsletter, two cassette tapes on Pat's four principles of success, as well as my first monthly giving card telling me that my gift would be used in accordance with Ezra 7:17-18.

I checked out Ezra 7. Thereby I learned that Pat plans to use my generous contribution to purchase "bulls, rams, and lambs." Don't they have livestock ordinances in Virginia Beach? No wonder the 700 Club reaches millions—you can smell it all the way to Washington, DC! If Pat is able to reach millions through the use of bulls, rams, and lambs, that's fine. But Ezra 7:18 troubled me because it tells Pat: "Whatever seems good to you and your brethren to do with the rest of the silver and gold, you may do."

I wrote and told my new buddy Pat that I would love to take credit for keeping his university afloat, the telephone lines open, Operation Blessing a blessing, a biblical consensus restored, and bulls, rams, and lambs off the street, but someone else had given the money in my name. If he would be kind enough to tell me who it was, I would like to pray for that person. I've got some things I'd like the Lord to do to him.

In answer to my letter, I received my December giving card asking for $15 or more to share the gift of eternal life.

One month's CBN newsletter informed me that Pat had designated his son Tim to be CBN's new president. I wrote Pat and asked why we members didn't get a chance to vote on Tim. In response, Pat sent my monthly giving card for March, asking for a sacrificial contribution to support his work. I felt better about Tim after I read in the newsletter how the Lord had once led him to give $1,000 to CBN just before his wedding, money he had been saving for his honeymoon. The next day, a man offered to send Tim and his new bride anywhere they wanted to go in the world. They honeymooned in Greece. How would I have learned all that without knowing Pat?

We went to Atlanta, Georgia, for our honeymoon.

Where do I find the person who enrolled me in the 700 Club and gave my name to someone named Gladys in Virginia Beach, who has been asking me for money? When I received my first personal correspondence from Pat, I thought not of rams and bulls in Ezra 7, but of the farmer whom Jesus describes in Matthew 13:24-30. Upon learning of the anonymous "gift" of some weeds amid his grain, the farmer observed, "An enemy has done this."

To the person who gave my name to Pat, whoever you are, wherever you are, know this: with a friend like you, I don't need enemies.

The Christian Ministry,
January–February 1988

82

Easter at Hope Church

As the hour approached 11 a.m., the bells pealed more exuberantly. A few choir members in white surplices and red cassocks began clustering in corners of the narthex. A reluctant acolyte—managed officiously by the Tzar of the Altar Guild and nemesis of generations of young males whose manipulative mothers forced the miscreants into acolyte service—was shoved toward the door leading into the sanctuary, pouting as he was thrust into duty.

"And put on those gloves," she ordered. "I don't give a rip whether you want to or not. Don't give me that look. No chewing gum!"

The senior managing pastor entered the narthex, smiling broadly to the choir who made way for His Eminence, planting a kiss on the cheeks of a couple of altos.

– 201 –

Secrets

"Hey, happy Easter to you!" snorted an older man in the narthex to no one in particular. Attired in an incongruous bright green vest, he spoke in a volume usually reserved for taverns.

"Shhhh!" the Tzar scolded, asserting her authority beyond pre-pubescent acolytes.

The organ gave way to the Hope Brass. Crucifer, clergy, and choir formed a line for the processional hymn. Preservice chaos gradually gave way to liturgical order. Dear old Herbert Cohellen, retired pastor who had settled at Hope, had been asked to march in the procession in order to make the announcements and to hand out the plates to the ushers at the offering, his chief liturgical sinecure. The pimple-faced crucifer continued to lean upon his cross—stolid, bored, as if to say to all, "I'm not really here." (His expression was not unlike a few in the choir.) The Hope Brass smothered all polite conversation in the narthex once the ushers opened the doors to the sanctuary.

"Tenors! Tenors!" shouted Gerald. "For God's sake, put yourselves in line. I need all of you if we're going to pull this off! Charles, all you basses look at me on that stanza when the anthem picks up steam! Look at me! Scott! That's you!"

"Let's do this thing, people," said the pastor jovially to the choir. He had regally emerged into the narthex, intoning cheerfully, "Break a leg, folks."

"Joe, give the high sign to Grimballs," ordered Gerald. (The choir-master referred to the organist as "Grimballs" behind his back.) A bass turned around and flipped a small switch. The organist having been cued, Easter ensued. "Showtime," Gerald said—in a voice that sounded like a near-pitch-perfect imitation of the late Orson Welles—as encouragement to the first wave of sopranos flowing into the aisle behind the crucifer. To the last in line he said, "Move it, honey," patting her rear with his chubby, perspiring hand.

Through doors held open by two ushers, the procession began to the strains of "Christ the Lord Is Risen Today." Ushers stood by with folding metal chairs, ready to sweep in behind the choir with additional seating. The congregation, which on most Sundays was half-hearted in its singing, now with pews packed, bordered on enthusiastic.

Christ the Lord has risen toda-ay, A-a-a-alelueea.

All rejoice and angels say-a, A-a-a-allelueea!

"Dum de dum, de dum dee dee," Gerald stood at the door, hammering out the tempo in the air for each successive wave of choristers. "Tenors, it's all up to you," his base threateningly boomed as they moved past. "Scott!"

With morning light streaming in the windows in a strong blue cast, the soaring arches, the well-ordered choir, noble organ, the brass interludes between the second and fourth stanzas, an eager, full house, Hope Church today approached the thrilling. Nor did energy flag as the service progressed—prayers well formed, elevated language fit to the occasion, a fresh new anthem, "Life! Life! Joy! Joy!" with tympani.

There was a collect, thanking God for life and the sun, the grass, and democracy. Then a selection from *Messiah*, keyed to the day. A scripture reading. Another hymn—a new one—that seemed to annoy some in the congregation with its unfamiliarity. A prayer of intercession by Herb in which God was informed of assorted health needs within the congregation and lectured on key current events. An acolyte nearly fumbled an offering plate when it was handed to him by the ushers; otherwise the production was flawless.

Herb struggled through the announcements, strategically placed in the middle to validate Hope as an active congregation. Someone really should get the announcements printed in large type if Herb was to be the usual announcer.

Women A'fire Bible Study Fellowship will not meet this week, due to Easter. But the Moving Men will meet this Wednesday to hear a presentation on "Ten Proofs of the Resurrection." Mick McConnell's famous sausage biscuits will be served. The winners of the Hope Happy Hearts Easter Bonnet contest are Agnes Youlonts and Mary Summers. Our "Send a Kid to Camp" drive begins next Sunday. Goal: one hundred indigent kids. And for those of you doing your spring cleaning, the clothes closet is in need of clean, warm winter coats in all children's sizes, even though it's April...

From here the service regained lost momentum and trotted toward the crescendo: the sermon by the managing pastor. The beginning of the Rev. Dr. Simon Lupino's sermon was (by skillful design) mildly disconcerting; the preacher began with a few dismal citations from the recent news about the decline of the economy, an earthquake in Asia, and a mass shooting at a mall somewhere in Texas, the failure of a hundred-year-old tire company in Akron, fare that few expected to be served in an Easter sermon. These unpleasantries were a rhetorical ploy. They poised the congregation for a good-hearted shove into the core of the message. A pause for a few silent seconds for effect, then:

Yet my friends, these stories of death, despair and mayhem are not the only story to be told. There is yet another word to be said. It is the word that has convened us this glorious Easter day—life!

Easter stories are charming and beloved—the women coming to a place of death, only to be surprised by life. The stupid disciples dumbfounded by glory. The announcing angel. I plead with you not to trouble yourselves with intellectual concerns about the mere facticity of these ancient texts, not to long for raw historical data.

Andante.

I want to reframe all that to reassure you that the word that these Bible stories are groping, in their own ancient ways, to speak, is a word more important than any of our misgivings about these primitive witnesses. As a great biblical scholar..., recently retired from an endowed chair at a university in Oregon, instructs us...

The preacher had forgotten the man's name.

These stories of the empty tomb are metaphor, a primitive way of expressing deeper, useful spiritual truth.

That message is as near to your souls as the word that our choir has sung so well—life! It is a word you are literally dying to hear. In the vale of the shadow of death—life! Immortal, unquenchable life!

His voice now raised to a high-pitched, earnest fortissimo.

Believe not those who tell you that you are a frail creature of constricted vistas and constrained future! Believe not the naysayers and negativists. Believe in life!

Easter is not about one Near Eastern man's unjust death and grim entombment. Injustice happens, particularly in that benighted part of the world. Easter is more. It is grand, cosmic, eternal, and indeed it is universal; most of all, it is relevant. It is the eternal message we hear whispered in our greatest poetry, our grandest music, and articulated in our wisest films—life!

Now a crescendo.

I do not stand before you to argue this, but rather to assert this— life!

This glorious day, with the sun shining down and the air fresh and clear, is eloquent natural testimonial to our supernatural theme— life!

Even as ex-president Jimmy Carter, man of malaise, has written,
we live in a "culture of death." The Easter word is a defiant protest
against that morbid world. And so, I boldly speak it to you in the
face of all your deadly, paltry "facts"—life!

Having risked a prophetic reference to Jimmy Carter at the end of
the first movement, the preacher now modulated his voice into a more
restrained, conversational tone as he told a story about a woman who
had feared that the successful, multimillion-dollar personal care prod-
ucts business she had founded in the basement of her home would fail
because of pressure from her creditors. A kind, charitable banker (who
was Jewish!) had found a way around restrictive government regulations
and had come to her aid with a bridge loan through which she was saved.

Life! Life! he resumed shouting at the top of his voice in grand, closing molto crescendo. *Liiife!*

Exeunt.

By prearrangement with the musicians, these last words of the sermon were immediately followed by a building roll of tympani, the jarring clash of cymbals, and the choir's near shouting of a verse adapted
from the old favorite, "He Lives!"

He lives! He lives! You ask me how I know he lives? He lives within
my heart!

A thrill ran through the congregation, their collective response
to this theatrical coordination between preacher and musicians. More
brass, another clash of cymbals, and the organ took up the first of "Up
from the Grave He Arose" as crucifer and clergy smoothly glided into
positions and the recessional began. Some in the choir, both women
and men, had tears on their cheeks as they walked and sang. Some
shouted more than sang. Despite the full service, the benediction was
pronounced by the senior managing pastor, followed by the Sevenfold

Amen, at a mere five minutes past noon, a testimonial to careful liturgical execution.

"Thanks for another grand service," more than one congregant was heard to say as the clergy glad-handed nearly everyone who exited, hugging some.

"What an Easter!" one portly, red-faced man in a plaid sport coat exclaimed.

The person who queried, "Did you mean to criticize or to praise Jimmy Carter? I never was much on Carter," was smilingly shoved on ahead and out the door.

Incorporation: A Novel,
Wipf and Stock Publishers, 2012

83
Feedback

In my seminary homiletics class, I invited a panel of local pastors to discuss the subject of preaching with the students. One student asked the panel, "How do you feel when people criticize your sermons?"

To the students' surprise, none of the pastors seemed to resent criticism of his or her preaching. "A sermon really begins when someone says, 'I didn't like what you said about so-and-so,'" explained one pastor. As far as preachers are concerned, any feedback, even negative, is better than none.

I suppose I should feel that way as a writer. The other day I was going through the thick file that I labeled "Response to Writing." If feedback is nourishment for a preacher, then I am well-fed. For instance, after "a practical magazine for thinking clergy" published my marvelously candid revelation about my pastoral relationship with Vanna White, someone wrote to the editor:

> To whom it may concern, if anyone. I just read your magazine. In particular, the article in the Last Word section. Question: IS THIS A JOKE? Is this star-stunned ding-dong really a pastor?

Following a soul-searching piece on canine evangelism, "My Dog, the Methodist," a bishop wrote to me:

> Unfortunately, the United Methodist Discipline does not allow me to touch you, but, if I were your bishop, I would have you in hot water before you could say "boo."

Or before I could say "bark"?

On another occasion, someone who identified herself as having "given a lifetime to peace and justice ministry" told me:

> Your article made me so mad I think that you ought to be shot. You have done great damage to the cause of peace in our church by your terrible ideas.

Pistol-packing pacifists.

Criticism of liberal theology won me this fusillade:

> No, Dr. Willimon, we will not march back into the dark ages of narrow-mindedness, bigotry, and closed thinking. If I had my way, you would be banished from the pages of every church magazine, defrocked and silenced.

Just imagine what he would do to me if he weren't open-minded.

In response to a book I wrote on denominational decline, someone said:

I agree that you are right on many of your points and, to a great extent, you are right. But I do not support your right to say these things in a book published by our own denomination.

Sometimes one doesn't have the right to write what is right.

Please keep those cards and letters coming. Preachers like me love to know that they are being heard. On second thought, just keep those cards and letters.

The Christian Ministry,
March–April 1988

84
Lecture Interrupted

When I began teaching, the dean thought it would be good for me to warm up to the vocation (after five years in the pastorate) by teaching in our summer school designed for those called into the pastoral ministry later in life. Many of these students have walked away from lucrative jobs. Many are already serving in some—shall we say—challenging congregations. Since they won't be going to seminary, the church requires them to spend five summers in our local pastors school.

I was lecturing on "effective liturgical leadership." Using some of Robert Hovda's thoughts on priestly ministry, I was stressing how the one who presides in the liturgy sets the tone and tenor for the assembly, conveys the church's faith in its acts of worship. A hand went up.

"Doc," said a large pastor from a small church in the hills of West Virginia, "I had something happen the Sunday before I come down here. Don't know if I handled it right or not. I was at the prayer time and so I asked the church, 'Do you have any special prayer needs?'

"A woman raised her hand and said, 'Yeah, I got one. I want you to pray that Mary Jones will stop leading my husband into adultery.' With that, Mary Jones jumped up, screaming, 'You bitch!' and the two of them locked in a fight, pulling and jerking each other all over the church. Their husbands got into it too, one ramming the head of the other into the backside of the pew."

I froze at the lectern, mouth agape. What got me more than his story was the class's reaction. All of the other students sat passively, some nodding in silent agreement, as if to say, "Yep, that same thing happened at my church just last week." Apparently, no one found anything that they were hearing to be ecclesiastically odd. Some appeared to be taking notes.

"So," he continued, "I come down out of the pulpit, pulled the two women apart, and said, 'Stop it! Sit yourselves back down. Now, I'm gonna ask one more time. Are there any prayer requests? And I'm gonna see if you can do it right this time. And if you people don't settle down and act like Christians, I'm gonna bust some heads. Ya'll is acting like that crowd Paul had to put up with in Corinth!'

"They knowed I could bust heads if I needed to. I was in the Marines before the Lord called me to seminary; also did a little pro wrestlin'. They quieted down and we went on with the service. Now, Doc, my question is, was this what you would call 'good liturgical leadership'?"

I mumbled, "That's precisely what I was talking about." Then I dismissed the class. I stumbled back to my office where I prayed, "Lord, help me to be a good seminary professor. I can't do this by myself."

The Christian Century,
February 13, 2002

85

Bama Bowl Bound, or My Van and Why I Got It

A Saturday morning fall a year ago, I woke up and, for some inexplicable reason, began browsing through the automobile advertisements in the *Herald*, looking at the ads for conversion vans. I couldn't believe they were so expensive, so I decided to forget about whatever it was that I was thinking when I inexplicably turned to the automobile section of the paper.

Then my wife, Patsy, said, "I know what you are looking for. I saw it on the lot last week, a used Duke Blue van."

Ten minutes later, we were at the car dealer looking at a Dodge van, two years old, with blue shag carpet, curtains with blue velour tiebacks and fender skirts.

"Mr. Williston," said the man on the lot, "unlike a lot of these conversion vans, this one is done in good taste. You don't see curtains with blue velour tiebacks in many of them. Nothing brings a family together like a van."

"How many miles does it get per gallon of gas?" I asked.

"Mr. Williamson," said the salesman, "as they says, if you got to ask, you can't afford it."

For some reason, all of this made perfect sense to me and so we bought it. One can expect decisions of this sort to arise out of a relationship like marriage that begins with two people who are perfect strangers deciding to live together for the rest of their lives. After that, anything is possible.

The next morning, we arose early and staggered downstairs, peering into our garage. To our genuine surprise, there was a blue-and-white van parked there, with curtains with blue velour tiebacks.

"We really did buy a van," I said in amazement. "What was I doing? Was I drunk?"

"Of course not," said Patsy. "You are a Methodist. Crazy, yes; drunk, no."

"Well, I'm going to drive that van when Duke is invited to play in a bowl," said I.

"You really are crazy," said Patsy. "First he buys a van with curtains and velour tiebacks, then he talks of going with Duke to a bowl."

The van took over our whole garage. We had to move the lawn mower, the dog, and everything else out to make room for the van. It was so tall that the garage door had to be propped up with a rake to get the thing in. I tore off one side of the garage door the second time I tried backing it in.

Still, it was Duke Blue. "I just can't get used to you in that van," said a woman as I climbed out of the van one Sunday before church. "It doesn't look right, somebody in a clerical collar driving that. Blue velour and black broadcloth just don't go together."

"Oh," said I, "I wouldn't know what to do without this van. It is very helpful in my work."

"What work?" she persisted.

"Well, I haul students in it," I said. "Take them to work for Habitat for Humanity, and on mission work teams to places in South Carolina."

"You use it to work out your middle-aged crisis," she said as she proceeded down the sidewalk.

"Besides, I'm going to drive that van to wherever Duke plays in a bowl, whenever we get asked to play in a bowl."

The woman kept walking, right on beyond the front door of the chapel and she didn't stop until she got to First Baptist.

The next Sunday, Dr. Jim Kelly was coming out of the chapel and said, in a jovial tone, "There is some student or someone parked in your parking place, this unbelievable blue van, even."

"That's my van," I said defensively.

"Your van!" exclaimed Jim. "That can't be. That thing has white stripes down the side, running boards, blue velour tiebacks."

"At least it is all done in good taste," I said.

"It is not. It is done in terrible taste. It looks ridiculous. You aren't having a breakdown, are you?"

"I'm driving it to the bowl, whenever we get invited to one," I said in a low, defiant tone.

"Bend over and let me take your temperature," said Dr. Kelly. "You're sick."

These are the sort of people with whom I have to work.

"Where did you get the money to buy that thing?" asked Charles Putman, vice president, the first time he saw the van. Charles is from Texas so I knew that he was just green with envy over the curtains with the blue velour tiebacks.

"Well," I explained, "I had an offer from a big church up east a few weeks ago. The president heard about it and immediately called to ask me what it would take to keep me at Duke. I told him that nothing would do except for a Duke Blue conversion van."

"With blue velour seats and shag carpet?" asked Charles.

"Right. So here it is," said I. "Besides, I'll be driving it to the bowl game, whenever Duke gets invited. You can go with me if you promise to act right." I knew that Charles was just eaten up with jealousy. People from Texas can't stand anybody to have anything bigger than what they have. That was all I heard out of Charles until a couple of days later when Duke beat Tennessee and there was a rumor abroad that another school was trying to hire away our coach.

Charles called me. "Look," he said, effecting a very officious tone of voice, "things have gotten tough in the negotiations to keep Coach Spurrier."

"So, what does that have to do with me?" I asked.

"Well, it finally got down to what would really make the coach happy, what would keep him here at Duke, and, well, I don't know how to tell you this, but, well, the president had to give him your van."

"My van!"

"Yes, and he's asked me to call you and ask you to drive it over to Allen Building. Leave the keys under the mat. He says he'll make it up to you somehow," said Charles. "The president says that he can get him a good preacher anytime he wants one, but a good football coach is scarce."

"Steve Spurrier isn't driving my van to the bowl—I am," I said.

"What bowl?" asked Charles.

"Just you wait," said I.

I drove my van through the rest of the fall, into the winter, spring, and summer. Somehow, during that period of time, I guess I got a little loose and invited a number of other people to ride in my van if we ever went to a bowl. It had become a joke around our house, the kind of thing that you sometimes say, like, "When I get a million dollars," or, "When they elect me king of Durham."

Then came this fall and our win over Northwestern. Then we beat Maryland. When we beat Clemson, it suddenly dawned on me that I had problems. People started coming up to me, people like Charles Putman, telling me that I had invited them to ride in my van to the bowl, people I don't even know, people who teach in the social sciences, even, all patting me on the back and saying things like, "Don't worry, I'll bring my cooler." I realized that, in various wild and unguarded moments, I had invited about half of Durham to ride in our van when we went to the bowl. When Ruth Ross called me and said that she preferred a window seat, I knew that the thing had gotten way out of hand. Of course, I never had any idea that I would actually have to make good on these offers.

At a party last week, two men actually got into a fight over which one had been invited first to ride in my van. I had a real moral dilemma on my hands. I had always talked about going to a bowl, but never dreamed we would. The only person I had ever met at Duke who had seen Duke play in a bowl had grandchildren.

My moral problem is but a microcosm to the sort of moral agony that is going on throughout the Duke campus because of our having such a good football team. For years Duke fans have been saying things like, "Football has been totally out of control in intercollegiate athletics; we are getting things back into perspective here at Duke" and "A university with the academic standing of Duke cannot expect to have a winning football team." In other words, we at Duke are too smart or too moral to have a good football team.

Now, what do we say? Steve Spurrier has made a lot of us have to do some circuitous ethical reasoning to explain why we are still smart and moral even though we thrashed Clemson. More than these moral problems, there is also the question of style. For years, Duke fans have looked with disdain upon the orange polyester leisure suits and painted-on tiger paws of the Clemson fans, the gaudy red of all those people from NC State. We sat there, losers with a superior smirk on our faces, dressed in tasteful tweed when they invaded Wallace Wade stadium.

We thought we were above all that. The problem was, we had not known what it was like to be invited to a bowl in Birmingham. When that happens, you find out that the only difference between you and somebody from Clemson who makes a fool out of himself at football games is lack of opportunity. For Christmas I'm asking for two blue flags to go on either side of the van and a Blue Devil tire cover for the rear (I got a pewter Duke license plate last Christmas) and an autographed picture of Clarkston Hines. As it turns out, gaudiness has nothing to do with intelligence or morality. It is a function of winning.

But my main point is to reiterate that Duke's road to the All-American Bowl began with that Saturday, two years ago, when I awoke and felt a need for a van. Steve Spurrier got Atlantic Coast Conference Coach of the Year, but I deserve something too. I was the first true believer, the first to make a concrete, visible (with blue velour tiebacks, no less) commitment to winning football. Even as they laughed at Noah building his ark before the flood, so they derided and ridiculed me fitting out my van for the bowl. Yet I kept the faith. I never wavered.

And right now, if Charles Putman came to me on bended knee and begged me like a child to ride with me in my van to Birmingham, I wouldn't let him. That goes for Jim Kelly too, and all the others. Steve can ride in my van if he wants to. Wave to us if we pass you on the road to Birmingham. We'll be in the van, the one with the Blue Devil tire cover, fender skirts, pewter Duke license plate, two Duke flags, and, yes, the blue velour tiebacks.

Duke Dialogue, November 1982

86
Pastoral Encounter

"I believe my latest bout began when my neighbor installed this mercury vapor light in her backyard. I don't have to tell you what those things do to a person's brain! My valic waves were out of sync something terrible! Couldn't sleep at night. Are you with me?"

I'm trying real hard to follow.

"Recycling is the only answer. Every aluminum can we save helps to restore the cosmic balance. Although glass, especially green glass, is better."

"You're losing me."

"Preacher, pay attention. What do they teach people in seminary these days? Well, it's been a long time since you were in seminary. I can't blame you. So many demands are made upon you. But you really have got to investigate the seriousness of mercury vapor lights. I think my neighbor is trying to torture me to death with hers. And if the Russians ever get them, what are we to do?"

Russians?

"I know that you hate George Bush..."

What?

"Don't lie to me! Anybody can figure out your politics just by listening to your sermons. You know not how to be subtle. But I feel I understand Mr. Bush. I feel I'm the only person in the world who could really help him."

"In what way could you help?"

"Well, it's obvious, isn't it? Like saying to him: 'Mr. Bush, I am sexualphobic myself.'"

Say what?

"Don't act so surprised. I wrote Mr. Gorby and told him about Mr. Bush's problem. It might help him negotiate for wheat and computers if he knows the sort of man he's dealing with and the cross he's bearing. If only Mr. Bush would reach out and ask for help. Does he have a pastor? But then, what good could a pastor do him? Right?"

Right.

"And another thing. What have you got against reincarnation? You're so big on ecology. Did it ever occur to you that people might treat their garbage differently if they knew they might come back as a bug in a solid waste dump?"

Never thought of that.

"I'm unsurprised that you are lagging behind. You have such a limited worldview."

Yes, yes, I do. I'm realizing I am limited.

"Still, you can't help it, can you? Limited and sheltered clergy. Did I ever tell you I once had an affair with James Brown's trumpet player?"

"No. I don't think you ever mentioned that to me." *Why do you save the good stuff 'till the end?*

"Well, I did have an affair. I was all dressed in red then, and I was wearing this wet, white turban on my head, to keep in my etheric forces, of course. As it turns out, we had known each other in a former existence and he recognized me. I didn't recognize him, but who could blame me for that? My astral body was totally out of control then. You know what I mean."

I do?

"I worry about you sometimes, preacher."

You worry about me?

"Well, here you sit, surrounded by mercury vapor lights, wires within computers. The sadly sexphobic. I worry about your etheric forces. No turban. No hat! It makes me wonder what you might have been in a previous existence. Sometimes it's just too much to think about."

Life is complicated, isn't it?

"Did I ever tell you I once had an affair with James Brown's trumpet player?"

"I believe you did."

The Christian Ministry,
January–February 1991

87

City of Bureaucratic Love

John Vannorsdall, president of Lutheran Theological Seminary at Philadelphia, has invited me to give a set of lectures. I would like to give them, and am honored to be invited, but due to my troubles with the law I may have to back out. I can't go to the city of Philadelphia.

This is because of a trip to New York City I took two years ago with my wife and children. What hath New York to do with Philadelphia? While in New York, we kept our gray Nissan sedan, North Carolina license plate number KKM 228, at the parking lot across the street from the hotel.

At the end of three days, we picked up our car—paying slightly more for the privilege of parking than we paid for a double room for the weekend, four theater tickets, and nine meals. At least the car had been safe, right?

Wrong. A month later, I got a letter from Philadelphia's police chief telling me that I owed him thirty dollars for illegally parking a gray Nissan sedan, North Carolina license plate number KKM 228, in Philadelphia. But the violation occurred the same weekend I was in New York. Obviously, the people who run the garage in New York are relatives of the folk at the Chicago garage in the movie *Ferris Bueller's Day Off*—why just park the car when they can take the car out for a spin?

I wrote to the chief and told him I hadn't been in Philadelphia that weekend. A month later he wrote to tell me that I now owed the people of Philadelphia sixty dollars, US currency, cashier's check only, no credit cards accepted. I wrote to him again, saying that there must be some misunderstanding—we are failing to communicate. A month later, the chief wrote to tell me to "understand" that my fine was now eighty dollars.

I called a lawyer. "You aren't corresponding with a chief of police; you're talking to a computer," he informed me.

"You're telling me," I said. "That rascal has 'computed' fifty more dollars in three months."

He told me not to worry about it. "The worst they could do is arrest you if you ever go to Philadelphia, ha ha!"

I wrote again, this time having my letter notarized to make it look more impressive and official. For this, I received another letter from the chief, declaring me a fugitive from justice. I was now a hunted man, on the lam.

Another letter from me elicited a letter from the Philadelphia Department of Public Service, saying that "all appeals for reconsideration of water bills should be addressed to Office 9-B-2, City Hall." What were they up to now?

I called my lawyer. "Don't worry," he said. "They can't touch you. But be careful if you ever change planes in the Philly airport. They might try to nab you, ha ha!"

Dear President Vannorsdall: I can't come to Philadelphia. It would be an ugly sight to have a Methodist minister dragged off the stage at Lutheran seminary while attempting to give a lecture titled "The New Hermeneutic Meets the New Homiletic." Although I, like W. C. Fields, would rather be in Philadelphia, I can't. Is it possible for this year's Lutheran lectures to be held at Sam's Truck Stop outside Trenton, New Jersey? And don't put my name on the brochure.

The Christian Ministry,
January–February 1989

88
At God's Disposal

My first attempt at a sermon was while I was a summer youth pastor at Trinity UMC in Anderson, South Carolina, '68. Of course, I attacked Lyndon Johnson (maybe Lady Bird too), and of course, I assailed the then-current Vietnam War.

After service, an enraged man shouted at the church door, "Punks like you are the shame of America" and "You are a cowardly little pussy who doesn't support our boys fighting in Southeast Asia."

"I'll have you know I was a Distinguished Military Student at Wofford," I protested. "You're looking at a second lieutenant, armor, though I never saw a tank." My lame defense served only to inflame. I was unsure whether to protect my face, my stomach, or my groin.

I staggered back into the church, getting as far as the vestry. A member of the altar guild, an older woman in a small, pink hat, was removing flowers from the brass vases.

"That was awful!" I gasped. "Did you hear what he said to me?"

"I think everyone heard," she said. "I do wish people wouldn't use such language when children are present. Could you hand me that container?"

"You and me both. He was going to hit me! How could that jerk be that upset by a first-year seminarian trying to preach?"

She looked up from fussing with flowers and said, "Dear, it's not you who upset him. I'm sure you remind him of his son. Both of you have long hair, though you appear to have no tattoos or ear piercing. Tommy is a homosexual, living in California or somewhere like that. He's lost the son to whom he gave his life. Tom kept his promise to God to be a good father, but God failed to keep his promise to Tom."

She laughed to herself. "Now, who would be upset with a nice boy like you? No, Tom hates *God*."

As I staggered out of the vestry, she said sweetly, "Everyone is so grateful that such a nice young man is willing to put himself at God's disposal. Good luck."

Accidental Preacher: A Memoir, William
B. Eerdmans Publishing Company, 2019

89

The Day Rev. Henderson Bumped His Head

Leaning down toward the bottom shelf to retrieve his trusty *Strong's Concordance* to pursue "new moon" through both testaments, the Reverend Henry Henderson, pastor of Sword of Truth Presbyterian Church, bumped his head.

"Darn," he exclaimed, grabbing his forehead. This he followed immediately with "Damn," sworn with atypical candor. The rather non-ministerial ejaculation surprised Henderson. Could he have actually said that? "Damn," he heard himself say again. "This hurts." That, so far as the Reverend Henderson could tell, was how it all began—an accidental blow to the brain while reaching for a concordance.

Moments later the phone rang. "Pastor," whined a nasal voice at the other end, "are you busy?"

"Not at all," said Henderson, out of habit. Then, from some mysterious depth in his soul, Henderson said, "I'm sitting here in my study, just dying for an emotionally needy person like you to call and make my day! No, I am busy. I was working on my sermon for next Sunday. What's your problem this time?"

His words paralyzed him. They must also have stunned the whimpering voice at the other end of the line, for there was a long, awkward silence followed by "Er, well, I'll call you at home tonight after work, Pastor."

"No," said Henderson firmly, alien words forming in his mouth as if not by his own devising, "call me during office hours on any day other than Friday. Thank you. Goodbye."

The receiver dropped from his hand and into the telephone cradle. He felt odd. Quite odd. His head no longer throbbed. Yet he felt odd.

Pastor in Peril

Emerging from his study, he encountered Jane Smith, come to church for her usual Friday duties for the altar guild. "As usual, just me," she said to Henderson. "They all say they'll be on the guild, that they don't mind helping out the church. Yet, when it comes time for the work, where are they?"

"I think you know very well why they are not here," said Henderson. "You gave them only a half-hearted invitation. Everyone knows you love playing the martyr. Their absence helps bolster your holier-than-thou attitude."

Smith nearly dropped the offering plate she was holding, along with the polishing cloth and the can of polish.

"Pastor! How dare you accuse me of being a complainer! You know how hard I've worked to get the altar guild going! If you gave us volunteers the kind of support we ought to..."

Henderson wasn't listening. He staggered down the hall as Jane Smith continued her complaint. He was feeling dizzy, unsteady.

Out in the parking lot, gasping for fresh air, Henderson was spied by John Tyler. "Glad I caught you," said John. "Pray for Florence. My wife is under the weather again. Just working herself to death, I think. She won't be at the finance committee meeting tonight. I'll tell her that you excused her."

"I doubt that Florence will know whether you told me or not, considering her 'condition,'" said Henderson to Tyler, making air quotes with his hands.

"What do you mean?" asked Tyler, mouth agog.

"You know what I mean. 'Under the weather' is your euphemism for 'dead drunk.' Denial is not just a river in Egypt, John. I've tried to broach the subject with you and Florence before. When you're ready to face the truth about Florence's habit, let me know. Until then, spare me the excuses."

Henderson got into his blue Toyota and slammed the door, leaving Tyler staring dumbly at him from the church walk. Seated behind the steering wheel, Henderson started the car and backed out quickly, as if he knew where he was going and what he was doing. He didn't. He was a man losing control. He simply could not stop telling the truth, no matter how much he wanted to do otherwise.

He was a pastor in peril.

From Bump to Prophet

Henderson at the hospital that afternoon, room 344: "So the doctor tells you your heart problems are congenital? That so? Are you sure the doctor didn't mention anything about (by my reckoning) eighty pounds of excess fat?"

And in room 204: "Really? So, this is the strain of emphysema that is not caused by smoking? Give me a break! Two packs a day for thirty years, and you wonder why you're sucking on an oxygen tank for dear life? Time to face the music."

At the finance committee meeting that evening: "Why wring our hands about the sad state of the budget? You don't need to be Einstein to figure this one out. I know very well that I am giving more to this church than anybody in the room tonight, and you know that I've got the lowest salary of anybody here—thanks to misers like you."

On Sunday, his last words to the frantic choir director, just before the procession began, were, or so it was reported, "Why worry about not having a couple of tenors? Will tenors redeem an anthem already ravaged by this so-called choir?"

After that fateful Sunday service, after a pastoral prayer in which Henderson admitted to God, "Most of us didn't really want to hear anything truthful you have to reveal to us, cowards as we are," an emergency meeting of the pastor/parish committee was called. Of course, Henderson was fired, or at least that was what Henderson afterward said the committee did. The committee officially stated, "In a show of Christian compassion and concern, we are offering Brother Henderson a month's worth of free counseling and rest so that he can ponder where the Lord will lead him next. We pray for him and wish him God's blessings in his new field of ministry—wherever that may be."

The now ex-Reverend Henderson would later claim, "That bump on the head made a prophet out of me, despite myself."

Although most members of Sword of Truth Church, for compassion's sake, never spoke his name in years to come, when Henderson's name was mentioned, someone would always ask, "Wasn't that the poor man who suddenly went kinda nuts?"

Leadership, Spring 1998

90
Felix Visits Church

Slamming doors and muffled voices. People shuffled in, murmuring as they took their habitual seats. The organ gurgled a prelude. An aged choir (four older women, two ancient men) chirped a tremulous call to worship, "Here We Are," sung with resignation.

The pastor appeared from a side door next to the choir loft and then disappeared in a chair behind the pulpit. All that could be seen of him was his spouting hair. Then a couple of hymns that Felix remembered from his childhood at Beulah Baptist in Salisbury. An offering was collected and Felix, noting dollar bills in the plate, discreetly crumpled in his ten-dollar bill, smiling at an elderly woman down the pew.

When an usher thrust the attendance pad at him, Felix dutifully signed with the blunt golf pencil that had been provided. He included his new address and checked "Desire a Visit," because there was no category for newcomers. On the "Prayer Concerns" line, he wrote, "'You are the way and the wayfarers'—*The Prophet*." He smiled as he stretched to his left to pass the pad to his sole companion in the pew, an older woman who glared at him as she received the pad, jerking it from his hand.

The pastor seemed as little interested in the subject of his sermon as the passive congregation. His text was from one of the Gospels, wherever Jesus says to "love your neighbor as yourself." The preacher announced, "This is what Christianity is all about. The whole point of Jesus, in case any of you were wondering."

Felix smiled. He saw himself as on a pilgrimage in search of the point of it all. He had ventured forth on an assignment that took him away from the narrow, negative, judgmental Christianity of Beulah Baptist, upwards into some new but as yet indistinct, graciously vague, neighborly spirituality. The preacher's declaration that the point was "love your neighbor as yourself" sounded like *The Prophet*.

The preacher's interest in his subject quickened. His voice rose as he pronounced that most people don't notice that Jesus stressed "as yourself" as the key to Christianity. "So 'love your neighbor' isn't the mush you people think it is. Self-love is the basis for all true love," claimed the preacher. "If you can't love yourself, lots of luck loving anybody else. Schopenhauer said that love does not let itself be forced. So there. I say unto you that love, like faith, isn't forced. No means no."

The preacher gave a giggle that was unreturned by the congregation.

Felix scarcely had time to turn over these arresting thoughts before the preacher sneered, "As my mentor, the great Arthur Schopenhauer, put so well, 'If we were not all so excessively interested in ourselves, life would be so uninteresting that none of us would be able to endure it.' Get it?"

Felix surreptitiously googled Schopenhauer. A German philosopher, he was surprised to learn. The preacher had a mentor, a philosopher. Felix also had a dead mentor. He liked a preacher who cited great people. He was trying to memorize quotes too, even though most people had forgotten Gibran.

The preacher mentioned "the insidious myth of altruism," and some other things, then carefully read, spitting the words, "Again, Schopenhauer: 'Truth is no harlot who throws her arms round the neck of him who does not desire her... She is so coy a beauty that even the man who sacrifices everything to her can still not be certain of her favors.'" A couple of older women toward the front turned toward one another and frowned.

Felix had encountered a co-intellectual. "Truth is no harlot who throws her arms round the neck of him who does not desire her..." Though Gibran probably would not put it that way, Felix liked the quote. He saved "truth is no harlot" to the notepad.

At the end of the service, Felix followed the pastor and an adolescent acolyte out the door of the sanctuary and into the entrance hall. A few loitered and chatted.

"Passing through?" the pastor asked as he shook Felix's hand. The man's coiffure sprouted in various directions, though in the noontide heat some of his hair was now plastered to his forehead. He wore a clerical collar and scuffed, brown shoes, neither of which Felix had seen on preachers back home.

"Actually, I've just moved to Galilee," Felix responded.

"What in God's name for?" asked the pastor.

I'm Not From Here: A Parable,
Wipf and Stock Publishers, 2015

91

Gifts from the Dead

"How come our church has got all these plaques stuck everywhere? On the windows, the pews, at the bottom of the pulpit, even the piano. Is that because these people paid for the right to have their names on a plaque just because they gave money to the church?"

An elder responded, "We've got these plaques there to remind boys like you that you didn't think up Jesus on your own. Somebody had to tell you, show you. None of this belongs to you by virtue of your birth."

Sweeping his hand over the expanse of the Buncombe Street Sanctuary, he declared, "Boy, you didn't come into the world owning any of this. The names of the dead are stuck everywhere to remind you that what you believe, your salvation, this church—gift. Gift all the way down.

"If this church had done it right, we would've nailed a plaque on your forehead: Here, Courtesy of Somebody Else."

92

Epistle to the Church Called Mainline

Behold I make all things new! Even you. How eagerly you began this century that you so confidently called "Christian." You organized to beat the devil, to build, to expand, to crusade, to reform, to grow. Quite a contrast to the way your century ends. You, who enjoyed thinking of yourselves as "mainline," got sidelined. Though you are averse to taking my Word literally, for my sake, and for yours, I hope that you will at least take these words seriously.

I, the One who so exuberantly turned water into wine at Cana, tire of your propensity to turn wine into water at your bureaucracies in Nashville, Minneapolis, and Louisville. The best thing about you is your past. What does that tell you? My, how you loved to organize and build! You made North America into the most thoroughly Protestant Christian place in the world. Hospitals, orphanages, schools, nursing homes, printing presses. You really took love of neighbor to a new level, and I'm grateful. And while I enjoyed dismantling sacred edifices rather than building them, you built some beautiful churches.

Give me *The Lutheran Hymnal* any day over most of those tasteless "praise choruses" of some of my evangelical friends.

Fosdick, Harkness, Peale, Steimle, Thurman, Achtemeier can preach for me anytime they like. I wish some of them would steer a bit closer to the Scriptures, but I'll speak to them individually about that. When you mainliners stop talking about me, your preaching tends to get moralistic and trite. I hate that. It wouldn't kill you to get back to the Bible.

You know me, I love to make the old-line new. If you will stick with me, I shall give you a future, new wineskins, and all that. I am Lord of life, not death. I shall move you from mordant decline to life. I've still got plans for you. You'll be smaller, but small can be good. Ask the Mennonites. You will no longer be in charge of the nation, if you ever were. Where the heck did you get the dumb idea that "American" was equivalent to "Christian"? Remember, the national church thing was your idea of church, not mine.

Get back to the basics, like worship, service, and witness. Don't mourn the downsizing of your bureaucracy. I'd rather my folk be in mission rather than sitting behind desks shuffling papers.

You were once good at mission. Now that much of North America has never heard of me, it's about time to start thinking again of yourselves as missionaries.

Your marginalization may be providential. I promise you renewal, not restoration. Many will be grateful for your mainline open-handedness, the way you manage to make room for such a wide range of faithfulness within your congregations, your confidence that the church is more than an isolated congregation, that I ought to have a "body," and that the witness of past saints is worth celebrating today.

Personally, I fear you tend to be open-minded to a fault. Latitudinarianism is you all over. I wish you would hire some theologians with some guts for a change. Can't you find something more fun for your senior citizens to do than General Assemblies, General Conferences, and Diocesan Conventions? Send 'em to watch the leaves change in Maine rather waste all that time voting and debating. I haven't attended a national church meeting in years. Why should you?

Some of your good ideas from the last century may need a decent burial so that I can work birth in you in the next.

One more thing. Please get out of the middle of the road! That's where all the accidents happen, theologically speaking, and where you find the carcasses.

Above all, remember this: I wasn't crucified for my moderation.

Christianity Today, October 25, 1999

93

The Inundating Deep

One of my favorite photos of my namesake, Will, is of the two of us, his second summer of life, on Will's first trip to the South Carolina coast. I'm leading into the surf at sunset one who only recently had learned to walk. I expected him to be afraid at his first meeting of the sea. He is no fear and all joy.

He holds my hand. In the photo, you can see only our backs, an old man stooping toward the child, the child eagerly pushing forward. You can't see, but I'll never forget, the smile on his face, Will's delight as he eagerly entered the waves at my encouraging "Jump!"

I love that photo's depiction of one of the great joys of aging—leading a little one toward the grand adventure of the wide world, gripping his hand reassuringly, egging him on to face into the wind and to leap the waves.

But yesterday, when I looked at that picture of the two of us—the little boy and the old man—it occurred to me that I had misread that moment. I, who always thought I was leading the child, saw that I was being led. Here at sunset, the sea, the vast eternity of time that was rushing toward him with promise, was ebbing away from me, taking from me all that I loved, including the little boy named for me.

He was all future; I was now mostly past. In truth, the little one, still fresh in the world, had me by the hand, encouraging me to make my way into the deep, departing. He begins life eagerly jumping forward. I clutch his tiny hand tightly, my last grasp of the future, at the end of day as I stagger uncertainly, unwillingly toward the engulfing, eternal sea.

Not long from now, he'll have to let go and venture on without me. His grip is not tight enough to rescue me from the encroaching dark, the inundating deep.

No cure for that but God.

Accidental Preacher: A Memoir, William
B. Eerdmans Publishing Company, 2019

94

Epiphany

Late afternoon, Lent 1975, after finally finishing my sermon, I locked up Trinity United Methodist and made my way across the churchyard to our tiny parsonage for supper. Across the yard I saw William looking out from the parsonage window, bouncing on the back of the sofa, waiting for me.

My heart sank when I turned and saw a young man, late twenties, perhaps early thirties, coming down the church walk. *Just my rotten luck.* These drifters passed through North Myrtle Beach. Their hard-luck stories differed, but all had the same ending, "Give me twenty-five dollars."

I'll head him off, give him a twenty, and be rid of him. Don't have it in me, this late in the day, to hear any more trumped-up tales of woe.

"Hello!" he called to me cheerfully.

"Hello."

"You're working late this afternoon, aren't you?"

"What can I do for you?"

"Not a thing, other than what you are already doing," he said. "Good work."

Odd comment.

"I just stopped by to tell you I think you are doing a great job here at Trinity."

"Is it Miami or Charleston that you need money to get to?" I asked with annoyance.

"Money? No," he laughed. "I just stopped by to tell you that I appreciate all you do to get the good news out to folks. Nice work. Your sermons rock."

I looked at him more carefully. He had a dark tan and was wearing khakis, scuffed loafers, and a green golf shirt. Izod. He didn't look crazy, though in this town, it can be hard to tell. I saw no hint of a weapon.

"Say," he continued, "do you get much time to read the Bible?"

"Er, uh, sure. I read Scripture every day," I answered.

So, this is his shtick. He's going to wear me down with chitchat before making the ask.

"What do you think of it?" he asked.

"Uh, the Bible? I like it. I think it's good," I said.

"Thanks! 'Course, I had some great folks working with me. Glad to see it's still in print! Right?" he said jovially, buddy-tapping me lightly on the arm.

"Right," I said, my throat tightening. I assessed him closely. He looked like he had just walked off the Gator Hole Golf Course.

"Let me guess what your favorite Gospel is. Luke! Am I right? I bet you like Luke as a writer, don't you?" he said. "What a cool job Luke did on the parables. Right?"

As if the busted fall stewardship campaign was not humiliating enough, now this.

"Hey, just wanted to stop by and thank you. I'm sure it's not easy in this town. Really appreciate your hard work. You're a go-getter. Pay no mind to the trustees. I'll bring 'em around, eventually. The jail ministry you guys started last year is going just great," he said, moving toward me as if to threaten a hug. "Don't worry about the stewardship thing. The money will come, I'm sure," he said patronizingly.

I took a step back. "Sorry, I didn't get your name."

"Oh, that's funny," he said, laughing. "Just Jesus to you, of course."

"Look, are you trying to be cute?" I asked.

"You think that's cute?" he responded, looking hurt. "Hey, don't want to keep you from the valuable work you are doing. But please, don't overdo it. Remember, Trinity is my problem, not yours. Help people; go ahead and preach; write; just be sure you have a good time."

"Uh, if you're Jesus, where are you headed?" I asked.

"Akron, Ohio," he said casually.

"Akron, Ohio?" I asked.

"Business," he responded.

He took my hand, drawing me uncomfortably close, giving off a slight whiff of garlic and cigarettes, and said, "Well done, friend."

I received his embrace as stiffly as if I were Richard Nixon being hugged by Sammy Davis Jr. Yet as I watched him head toward the highway, I thanked God for my credulous childhood, for gates that opened and for voices that spoke in the haunted woods off Fork Shoals Road, and also for some proficiency in dealing with the comings and goings of a God both friendly and mischievous. He bounded toward Highway 17 North, where he gave me a wave, then hitched a ride from a green Toyota, and vanished toward the sunset.

That evening at supper, I related my epiphany to Patsy, just as I have told it to you. She chided me for wasting time cajoling a sadly deluded young man. I defended my actions. When one works a while with Jesus, one chastens one's notions of delusional.

Later that night, Patsy stood in our miniature bedroom, thoughtfully holding her toothbrush, and said, "One thing still bothers me. Why Akron, Ohio?"

On a Wild and Windy Mountain and
25 Other Meditations for the Christian Year,
Abingdon Press, 1984

95

Dawn Shall Break upon Us

1972, in Clinton, South Carolina, I learned how God is among us. We were preparing for the Christmas Eve communion service over at All Saints Church, to be led by Allan Warren, the town's eccentric Episcopal priest. (Is there any other kind?) Those of us in the so-called nonliturgical churches tend to use "liturgical" churches on occasions like Christmas Eve, when we're in the mood for a proper celebration.

Anticipating Allan's sermon, bolstering myself with one last cup of eggnog, I was "getting into the Christmas spirit," as they say.

Then came the news. The peace talks had stalled. Nixon had ordered massive bombing in North Vietnam. Anger and resentment surged within me. What right had Nixon to do this to our celebration? A sick, twisted, ironic way to note the birth of the Prince of Peace—not with the songs of angels unto shepherds but with screaming bombs over bamboo villages. Was a brief cease-fire too much for us peace wishers to ask?

I phoned Allan. Had he heard? Yes. What should be our response? After all, two of the town's most influential angry young pastors ought to say something! Would he mention the bombing in his sermon tonight? "I don't think we ought to let Nixon get away with it," I said. "We ought to blast him for it." Allan agreed. "A situation like this calls for a firm response—something radical, arrogant, even defiant." I braced myself for a major antiwar protest.

"There is only one thing to be done," he declared. "We must pull out all the stops tonight and praise God as never before."

What?

"Can you imagine anybody up at the Pentagon singing a Benedictus?" was Allan's only reply.

Sometimes the eccentricity of Episcopalians is too much. And so, not understanding, I trudged through the crisp December night to the little church where the organist was already struggling valiantly with a prelude, and a congregation of thirty or so waited in silence for the eleventh hour. When the hour arrived, in burst Allan in his tippet and biretta, accompanied by two disheveled adolescent acolytes. He made a couple of flourished bows to the altar, shifted his chasuble, and then, leaning over the chancel rail, with a mischievous twinkle in his eye, whispered to the congregation, as if letting us in on some secret that only he knew, "Tonight, the Lord God of Israel has come to set his people free."

I couldn't tell you exactly what took place during the rest of the service. Revelation had caught me off guard, and I was thrown into a kind of "minor ecstasy," as the Quakers say. I remember a couple of great old Advent hymns sung with as much propriety as Episcopalians can sing. I remember the passing of the peace and the iron-fisted grip of an octogenarian. I remember the smell of the wine and the taste of the bread, and I remember the choking clouds of incense that emanated from the censer of an overzealous—if not malicious—acolyte.

But mostly I remember old Zechariah's Benedictus sung lustily, off-key, and yes, "arrogantly and defiantly," by Allan, with the rest of us faint hearts joining in as best we could:

Blessed be the Lord God of Israel;

for he hath visited and redeemed his people

and hath raised up a mighty salvation for us...

Through the tender mercy of our God

Whereby the dayspring from on high hath visited us;

To give light to them that sit in darkness and in the

shadow of death,

and to guide our feet into the way of peace.

You see, the peculiar defense of Christians in the face of the world's darkness is often best expressed through a most relevant kind of holy irrelevance. My "response" to the bombing horror was little better than the horror itself—my resentment, my self-righteousness, merely echoed back in the face of a violent world. The Pentagon generals and I did share something after all: brothers in darkness we were.

And then came Allan, defiant, letting us in on the secret of the ages, supremely confident in the face of all evidence to the contrary, accompanied by a small boy swinging a smoking pot, leading us forth from the little church into the midnight air, bellowing forth "Joy to the World" at the top of our voices to anybody who had ears to hear.

The world cannot understand this hope of which we sing on Christmas Eve. In our more worldly moments, we do not understand this hope. But that night, for one fleeting, radical, scandalous, arrogant, defiant moment, I understood. With my eyes opened by incense and my appetite for joy whetted by a little bread and wine, and my hand still aching from the grip of a wise old woman who opened my clenched fist, all evidence in this barren silent night to the contrary, by the grace of God and Father Allan's priestly act, I praised God and joined with old Zechariah, who sang before his expectant wife:

> *"The dawn from heaven will break upon us,*
>
> *to give light to those who are sitting in darkness*
>
> *and in the shadow of death,*
>
> *to guide us on the path of peace." (Luke 1:78-79)*

The Christian Century,
December 5, 1979

96

Preacher to the Preachers

A few years ago, during the crisis in Lebanon, a reporter was interviewing the few Americans remaining in Beirut. The hostage crisis had prompted President Reagan to order all Americans out of the country. But the reporter had found an older woman, a Southern Baptist missionary, who wasn't leaving.

"The president did not send me here," she told him pleasantly. "I'm here at the behest of the Southern Baptist Foreign Mission Board."

"The State Department has said that it cannot guarantee the security of Americans in Lebanon," countered the reporter.

"From what I can see, the State Department hasn't made us very secure here at any time," she said with a twinkle in her eye. "My safety is not based upon the State Department."

"Don't you have family in the US?" persisted the reporter. "If you stay, you will be arrested and fined when you return to the US."

"Yes, I have family. Would you like to see pictures of my grandchildren? But the people of Lebanon are also my family. Do you think the American government is going to arrest a grandmother going through customs at Kennedy Airport? Besides, the case would be tied up in the courts until I die. I still have much work to do for Christ. I'm staying."

Some preacher helped produce that woman. When you spoke the Word, she heard her name called, she came forth, she resisted and she persisted. She is living proof of the continuing power of the gospel. If you get depressed about the quality of your ministry (and what preacher doesn't?), take heart. She and others like her are the validation of our homiletical efforts, evidence that we have not preached in vain.

The Christian Ministry,
September–October 1995

Story Title Index

Scripture Index

Theme Index

Credits

"Father's Day" comes originally from "The Unfettered Word," sermon, Duke University Chapel, October 15, 1989. It is reprinted by permission of the publisher from *The Collected Sermons of William H. Willimon* (Louisville, KY: Westminster John Knox Press, 2010) where it originally was seen in print.

"What I'm Trying to Say Is..." is reprinted by permission of the publisher from *The Last Word: Insights About the Church and Ministry* (Nashville: Abingdon Press, 2000).

"Sent" is reprinted by permission of the publisher from *Accidental Preacher: A Memoir* (Grand Rapids, MI: William B. Eerdmans Publishing Company, 2019).

"Sermon Slips" is reprinted by permission of the *Christian Century* from the November–December 1988 issue of the *Christian Ministry*.

"School" comes originally from "Jesus Goes to School," sermon, Duke University Chapel, December 22, 1991. It is reprinted by permission of the publisher from *The Collected Sermons of William H. Willimon* (Louisville, KY: Westminster John Knox Press, 2010) where it originally was seen in print.

"Who's the King?" comes originally from "Who's in Charge Here?" sermon, Duke University Chapel, November 22, 1992. It is reprinted by permission of the publisher from *The Collected Sermons of William H. Willimon* (Louisville, KY: Westminster John Knox Press, 2010) where it originally was seen in print.

"In the Presence of a Prophet" is reprinted by permission of the publisher from *Accidental Preacher: A Memoir* (Grand Rapids, MI: William B. Eerdmans Publishing Company, 2019).

"Successful Preaching" is reprinted by permission of the publisher from *The Last Word: Insights About the Church and Ministry* (Nashville: Abingdon Press, 2000).

"Is Jesus Serious?" comes originally from "Only a Savior Like Jesus Could Love People Like You," sermon, Duke University Chapel, September 18, 2011.

"Send a Preacher to Camp" is reprinted by permission of the *Christian Century* from their November 8, 1989 issue.

"I Was Vanna's Pastor" is reprinted by permission of the *Christian Century* from the January 1987 issue of the *Christian Ministry*.

Preacher: A Memoir (Grand Rapids, MI: William B. Eerdmans Publishing Company, 2019).

"The Blessing of Assignment" is reprinted from *How Odd of God: Chosen for the Curious Vocation of Preaching* (Louisville, KY: Westminster John Knox Press, 2015).

"On the Jericho Road" comes originally from a sermon by the same name, Trinity United Methodist Church, September 15, 1974. It is reprinted by permission of the publisher from *The Collected Sermons of William H. Willimon* (Louisville, KY: Westminster John Knox Press, 2010) where it originally was seen in print.

"Fathers and Sons Needed Deliverance from the River" is reprinted by permission of Duke University from the September 1987 issue of the *Duke Dialogue.*

"Vocative God" is reprinted by permission of the publisher from *Accidental Preacher: A Memoir* (Grand Rapids, MI: William B. Eerdmans Publishing Company, 2019).

"Savior" comes originally from "On the Jericho Road," sermon, Trinity United Methodist Church, September 15, 1974. It is reprinted by permission of the publisher from *The Collected Sermons of William H. Willimon* (Louisville, KY: Westminster John Knox Press, 2010) where it originally was seen in print.

"Two People at Prayer" comes originally from "Pharisees and Publicans All," sermon, Duke University Chapel, October 26, 1986. It is reprinted by permission of the publisher from *The Collected Sermons of William H. Willimon* (Louisville, KY: Westminster John Knox Press, 2010) where it originally was seen in print.

"Come, Join the Party" comes originally from "The Judgment of Grace," sermon, Battelle Chapel, Yale University, October 9, 2011.

"Good Friday" is reprinted by permission of the publisher from *Why Jesus?* (Nashville: Abingdon Press, 2010).

"Confirmed" is reprinted by permission of the publisher from *Accidental Preacher: A Memoir* (Grand Rapids, MI: William B. Eerdmans Publishing Company, 2019).

"Jews and Christians, All in the Family" comes originally from a sermon of the same name at Duke University Chapel, December 7, 1986. It

Credits

"Unto Us a Child" is reprinted by permission of the *Christian Century* from their December 19, 1979 issue.

"Great Moments in Worship" is reprinted by permission of the *Christian Century* from the March 1987 issue of the *Christian Ministry*.

"Before Us Good People" is reprinted from *What's Right with the Church: A Spirited Statement for Those Who Have Not Given Up on the Church and for Those Who Have* (New Orleans: Insight, 1998).

"Easter Proof" is reprinted by permission of the publisher from *A Peculiar Prophet: William H. Willimon and the Art of Preaching* (Nashville: Abingdon Press, 2004).

"The Joy of Being a Sinner" is reprinted by permission of the publisher from *Pastor: The Theology and Practice of Ordained Ministry* (Nashville: Abingdon Press, 2002).

"Olympics for Clerics" is reprinted by permission of the *Christian Century* from their November 23, 1983 issue.

"Best Little Harlot's House in Jericho" is reprinted by permission of the *Christian Century* from their October 26, 1983 issue.

"Bless You, Mrs. Degrafinried" is reprinted by permission of the *Christian Century* from their March 14, 1984 issue.

"Partners in Ministry" is reprinted by permission of the *Christian Century* from the January–February 1988 issue of the *Christian Ministry*.

"Easter at Hope Church" is reprinted by permission of Wipf and Stock Publishers, www.wipfandstock.com from *Incorporation: A Novel* (Eugene, OR: Wipf and Stock Publishers, 2012).

"Feedback" is reprinted by permission of the *Christian Century* from the March–April 1988 issue of the *Christian Ministry*.

"Lecture Interrupted" is reprinted by permission of the *Christian Century* from their February 13, 2002 issue.

"Bama Bowl Bound, or My Van and Why I Got It" is reprinted by permission of Duke University from the January 22, 1993 issue of the *Duke Dialogue*.

"Pastoral Encounter" is reprinted by permission of the *Christian Century* from the January–February 1991 issue of the *Christian Ministry*.

Credits

"City of Bureaucratic Love" is reprinted by permission of the *Christian Century* from the January–February 1989 issue of the *Christian Ministry*.

"At God's Disposal" is reprinted by permission of the publisher from *Accidental Preacher: A Memoir* (Grand Rapids, MI: William B. Eerdmans Publishing Company, 2019).

"The Day Rev. Henderson Bumped His Head" is reprinted by permission of *Christianity Today* from the Spring 1998 issue of *Leadership*.

"Felix Visits Church" is reprinted by permission of Wipf and Stock Publishers, www.wipfandstock.com from *I'm Not From Here: A Parable* (Eugene, OR: Wipf and Stock Publishers, 2015).

"Epistle to the Church Called Mainline" is reprinted by permission of *Christianity Today* where it originally appeared with the title "To the Church Called Mainline," October 25, 1999.

"The Inundating Deep" is reprinted by permission of the publisher from *Accidental Preacher: A Memoir* (Grand Rapids, MI: William B. Eerdmans Publishing Company, 2019).

"Epiphany" is reprinted by permission of the publisher from *On a Wild and Windy Mountain and 25 Other Meditations for the Christian Year* (Nashville: Abingdon Press, 1984).

"Dawn Shall Break upon Us" is reprinted by permission of the *Christian Century* from their December 5, 1979 issue.

"Preacher to the Preachers" is reprinted by permission of the *Christian Century* from the September–October 1995 issue of the *Christian Ministry*.